# Sasha Kagan's
# Classic Collection

# Sasha Kagan's
# Classic Collection

The Taunton Press

**The Taunton Press**
Inspiration for hands-on living®

The Taunton Press, Inc., 63 South Main Street, PO Box 5506,
Newtown, CT 06470-5506
email: tp@taunton.com

First published 2011 by
**Guild of Master Craftsman Publications Ltd**
Castle Place, 166 High Street, Lewes,
East Sussex BN7 1XU

The publishers and author can accept no legal responsibility for any
consequences arising from the application of information, advice or
instructions given in this publication.

**Publisher**  Jonathan Bailey
**Production Manager**  Jim Bulley
**Managing Editor**  Gerrie Purcell
**Senior Project Editor**  Virginia Brehaut
**Managing Art Editor**  Gilda Pacitti
**Art Editor**  Rebecca Mothersole
**Photography**  Chris Gloag

**Library of Congress Cataloging-in-Publication Data**

Kagan, Sasha.
  Sasha Kagan's classic collection / Sasha Kagan.
    p. cm.
  "First published 2011 by Guild of Master Craftsman Publications Ltd,
  Castle Place, 166 High Street, Lewes, East Sussex BN7 1XU."
  Includes index.
  ISBN 978-1-60085-411-8
  1. Knitting--Patterns. I. Title. II. Title: Classic collection.
  TT820.K256 2011
  746.43'2--dc22
                              2010053846

Set in interstate
Colour origination by GMC Reprographics
Printed and bound in China by Hung Hing Offset Ltd

# Contents

# Introduction

'The art that is frankly decorative is the art to live with. It is, of all visible arts, the one art that creates in us both mood and temperament...The harmony that resides in the delicate proportions of lines and masses becomes mirrored in the mind. The repetitions of patterns give us rest. The marvels of designs stir the imagination'
OSCAR WILDE  *The Artist as Critic*

WRITING THIS BOOK HAS BEEN QUITE AN EPIC JOURNEY. Thanks to a grant from Chance to Create and the Welsh Arts Council I have been able to look back over the past four decades of my design career and trace the thread of serendipitous circumstances that have shaped my creative path. Little did I realize, as I scraped away at my etching plates and carved patterns from wood blocks at the Royal College of Art, that one day I would translate my obsession with pattern into wearable art! With hindsight I realize that it was as much the love of the craft process and the joy of making by hand that fired my imagination; so not such a huge leap from inking up a plate to make a print to knitting and purling to make patterned fabric.

I have certainly had my fair share of luck along the way: an introduction to Joan Burstein, who gave me my very first order for six slipovers for Browns in South Molton street back in the 1970s; Vanessa Denza, who introduced me to exclusive American boutiques and department stores; Lady Philipa Powell of the Chelsea Craft Fair and Anne Stirling, who became my American agent and had me dressing big names in Hollywood (quite a boost for a small cottage industry based in Mid Wales); Amy Carroll, editor of my first book; and Trisha Malcolm who has commissioned many and various designs for *Vogue Knitting* magazine and the Soho publishing company.

Being a self-employed knitwear designer, mother of four children and living in a ridiculously remote location, I quickly had to learn how to juggle and ride the fickle waves of fashion. The early years of large-scale hand-knit production thankfully diversified into writing books of knitting patterns (the collections could then be offered to the home knitter to make for themselves). The books led on to teaching tours in the UK, USA, Australia and Japan. Yarn companies such as Rowan commissioned designs and *Vogue*, *Interweave Knits*, *Woman's Weekly*, *Woman's Realm*, *Knitting* and *The Knitter* all liked my look and asked for exclusives.

Exhibitions and shows also played a major part and provided venues to showcase my work. The Arts Council of Wales sponsored my first solo exhibition to coincide with the publication of *The Sasha Kagan Sweater Book* in 1984. This seminal show got lots of needles clicking and helped fuel the knitwear revolution. My second book *Big and Little Sweaters* was launched at the first ever Knitting and Stitching Show in the Rainbow rooms at Derry and Toms, followed by a very 1980s-style exhibit at Aberystwyth Arts Centre, Wales. My proudest moment was the launch of *Country Inspiration* at the Victoria and Albert Museum, London, in 2000 – to feel that I was a part of the great decorative arts tradition as exemplified by my all-time hero William Morris and the Arts and Crafts movement and that I was helping to elevate the noble craft of hand knitting gave me great satisfaction.

'My Life in Textiles – Four Decades of Classic Hand Knit Design' opened at Llantarnham Grange Arts Centre, Cwmbran, Wales, in November 2010 and will continue its tour of galleries and shows with a view to inspiring the next generation. This book and the exhibition have evolved side by side and I hope that I have sourced the essence of each decade for you in my choice of designs. Long may the craft flourish and evolve!

Happy Knitting!

*Sasha Kagan*

# Gallery of designs

## PART ONE: 1969–1979

**Silver birch scarf**

page 56

**Dotty short-sleeved
sweater**

page 58

**Spot tuxedo waistcoat**

page 62

**Mosaic V-neck slipover**

page 66

**Cherry shawl**

page 70

## PART TWO: 1980–1989

**Scotty dog sweater
and beret**

page 80

**Prowling cats sweater**

page 84

**Bavarian flower beanie
& fingerless gloves**

page 88

**Acorn shawl-collared
jacket**

page 90

**Lavender jacket**

page 94

# PART THREE: 1990–1999

**Tulip peplum jacket**

page 104

**Pansy pashmina**

page 108

**Wildflower cropped cardigan**

page 112

**Hazelnut V-neck jacket**

page 116

**Oriental flowers kimono**

page 120

# PART FOUR: 2000–2009

**Ivy hooded coat**

page 130

**Elderflower body-warmer**

page 134

**Sweet William sloppy joe**

page 138

**Carinthia tunic**

page 142

**Lichen bolero**

page 146

GALLERY OF DESIGNS

*This page and opposite:* **Silver birch scarf** page 56

*This page and opposite:* **Dotty short-sleeved sweater** page 58

*This page and opposite:* **Spot tuxedo waistcoat** page 62

*This page and opposite:* **Mosaic V-neck slipover**  page 66

*This page and opposite:* **Cherry shawl** page 70

*This page and opposite:* **Scotty dog sweater and beret** page 80

*This page:* **Bavarian flower beanie & fingerless gloves** page 88

*Opposite page:* **Prowling cats sweater** page 84

*This page and opposite:* **Acorn shawl-collared jacket** page 90

*This page and opposite:* **Lavender jacket** page 94

*This page and opposite:* **Tulip peplum jacket** page 104

*This page and opposite:* **Pansy pashmina** page 108

*This page and opposite:* **Wildflower cropped cardigan** page 112

*This page and opposite:* **Hazelnut V-neck jacket** page 116

*This page and opposite:* **Oriental flowers kimono** page 120

*This page and opposite:* **Ivy hooded coat** page 130

*This page and opposite:* **Elderflower body-warmer** page 134

*This page and opposite:* **Sweet William sloppy joe** page 138

*This page and opposite:* **Carinthia tunic** page 142

*This page and opposite:* **Lichen bolero** page 146

Knitted in Twilley's Cortina Super Crochet Wool

Four decades of classic hand-knit design

# A stitch in time

**JILL PIERCY**, CURATOR OF THE 'MY LIFE IN TEXTILES' EXHIBITION, SUMMARIZES SASHA'S EARLY YEARS AND EXTENSIVE CAREER.

Sasha Kagan originally trained as a painter at Exeter College of Art and then studied printmaking at the Royal College of Art. 'I made prints filled with pattern, woodcuts, lithographs and silk screens based on natural forms and various knitting stitches. My mother was a great knitter and professional needlewoman and an inveterate hoarder of scraps of yarn and fabric. From her I learnt to believe that knitting in many ways represents the ultimate in endeavour and application, and I feel lucky to have taken up the craft in our increasingly technological age at a time when it is becoming more appreciated and sought after.'

Sasha's knitwear career began while she was still at college. Her 1960s-style tank top designs were snapped up by Twilley's and *Woman's Own* magazine commissioned her colourful 1940s retro sweaters. After college she designed costumes for The Black Box Theatre Company, continued to explore knitting and taught printmaking. When the theatre company moved to the Welsh borders she decided to move too and has lived in Wales ever since.

**Opposite:** Sasha Kagan wearing her Optical Silver design, 1973.

**Above left:** *Twilley's* pattern 1971.
**Above right:** *Woman's Own* cover, 1974.

In 1977 she was awarded a Welsh Arts Council bursary to set up a dye workshop and began organizing her cottage industry with four outworkers. The business quickly grew and soon she had outlets in London, Milan, Berlin, New York and San Francisco and by 1984, she had 130 outworkers all over Britain knitting her designs. In that same year her first book of knitting patterns *The Sasha Kagan Sweater Book* (Dorling Kindersley, 1984) was published and she had her first solo touring exhibition. The book became so popular that it was re-published the following year in the USA, Japan and Spain.

# 'I feel lucky to have taken up the craft in our increasingly technological age at a time when it is becoming more appreciated and sought after.'

**Below left:** An early Memphis-inspired geometric design, 1969.

Her next book *Sasha Kagan's Big and Little Sweaters* (Dorling Kindersley, 1987) included patterns designed for children as well as adults and featured more of her witty and whimsical designs such as the flower girl and cowboy as well as florals and the Memphis-inspired geometrics.

She continues to produce two collections of new knitwear designs each year, exhibits widely, has regular international lecture tours, is a contributor to many knitting magazines and makes kits to enthuse knitters. Her textile career has been regularly punctuated with the publication of innovative pattern books. Inspiration for designs comes from many sources ranging from vintage knitting patterns to the flowers and leaves she sees from her studio window to embroidered textiles she finds on her travels.

**Below centre, right and far right:** Front cover and pages from *The Sasha Kagan Sweater Book*.

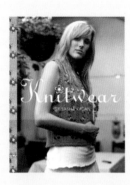

**Above:** The front cover of *Knitwear*, Sasha Kagan's 2008 book.

Sasha's early geometric designs were inspired by her love of Fair Isle sweaters from the 1940s and the rich and intricately patterned cardigans and slipovers crafted by her mother and aunt. Her designs began as small squares, triangles, spots and zigzags and she went on to explore the three-dimensional shapes that had been a recurring theme in her art-school days. Her love of geometry can often be seen as a subtle sub-layer in many of her patterns.

Sasha's passion for both gardening and the countryside has inspired many of her designs across all four decades of her career. *Country Inspiration* (Taunton Press, 2000) contains an extensive collection of 45 nature-inspired pieces and was accompanied by an exhibition at the Victoria and Albert Museum. As the colour of leaves alters through the seasons Sasha selects yarn to reflect the changes, from the vibrant lime greens of spring to the rusts and mellow yellows of autumn.

Her palette is very versatile and a collection is often based on a particular range of colours and yarns. Many of her patterns are based on her interest in folk design and traditional peasant costume. Tiny all-over repeating motifs, borders that lead into geometric scatterings of flowers, paisley swirls and floral fantasies are set in bright shades on a dark background, giving each garment a richness and depth.

Delving into the world of 'how-to' books, Sasha wrote *Knitting for Beginners* (Carroll & Brown, 2004). Crochet had always been present in Sasha's work as a way of finishing garments with an accent of colour or with a picot or shell edging. It came into its own with the book *Crochet Inspiration* (Sixth & Spring, 2007) where Sasha explores techniques and shapes that can be combined to create many garments, wraps and decorative themes. *Knitwear* (GMC Publications, 2008) followed, with a collection of re-worked favourites and new designs.

Her latest retrospective exhibition 'Sasha Kagan – My Life in Textiles' began its tour in autumn 2010. It became obvious very early on that the exhibition needed to be based around Sasha's main recurring motifs rather than be chronological. Together, we identified them as geometrics; her 'witty and whimsical' figurative designs; folkloric based on ethnic designs and traditional costumes; florals, leaves and the new range of abstract designs based on the close-up studies of mosses, lichens, slate and crystals.

In exploring Sasha's vast collection of garments and designs, it became clear that the majority of her designs are based on timeless shapes and the patterns, which can be interpreted in many colourways, can easily adapt to any decade and remain fresh and classic in the ever-changing world of fashion.

'AN AMAZING DECADE OF INTOXICATING CREATIVITY
- THE FASHION ANARCHY OF THE HIPPY GENERATION
KNEW NO BOUNDS.'

**1969–79**

The Silver birch design was first created in 1969. It featured in *Women's Wear Daily*, was knitted up for babywear and Brioche rib jackets and now reappears as a classic ribbed scarf.

# Silver birch scarf

**Sizes**
One size
**Width**
12in (30.5cm)
**Length**
93in (236cm)

**You will need**
Jamieson & Smith Shetland wool
2-ply jumper weight
(129yds/118m per 25g ball)
4 balls 1280 **Pale Green Mix (A)**
3 balls FC51 **Lilac Mix (B)**
3 balls FC56 **Purple Heather (D)**
3 balls FC37 **Blue Mix (F)**
2 balls FC50 **Rose Mix (C)**
2 balls 141 **Teal (G)**
2 balls 122 **Bracken (H)**
2 balls 202 **Oat (I)**
1 ball FC22 **Bright Pink (E)**
1 pair 3.25mm (US4:UK10) needles

**Tension**
25 sts and 32 rows to 4in (10cm) over stripe pattern after heavy pressing. *Use larger or smaller needles if necessary to obtain correct tension.*

## Pattern notes

5 x 5 rib – multiple of 5 + 5
**RS rows:** *K5, p5; rep from * to last 5 sts, k5.
**WS rows:** *P5, k5; rep from * to last 5 sts, p5.

## To make scarf

Using 3.25mm needles and A, cast on 75 sts.
Working in k5, p5 rib follow stripe sequence:
**Rows 1–10:** Pale Green Mix
**Row 11:** Bright Pink
**Rows 12–13:** Rose Mix
**Row 14:** Blue Mix
**Rows 15–19:** Oat
**Rows 20–21:** Blue Mix
**Row 22:** Oat
**Row 23:** Bright Pink
**Rows 24–26:** Pale Lilac
**Rows 27–28:** Bright Pink
**Rows 29–33:** Pale Lilac
**Rows 34–35:** Bracken
**Rows 36–39:** Purple Heather
**Rows 40–41:** Rose Pink
**Row 42:** Bright Pink
**Row 43–44:** Rose Pink
**Rows 45–47:** Purple Heather

**Rows 48–49:** Bracken
**Rows 50–54:** Pale Lilac
**Rows 55–56:** Bright Pink
**Row 57:** Rose Pink
**Rows 58–59:** Pale Lilac
**Row 60:** Rose Pink
**Row 61:** Oat
**Rows 62–63:** Blue Mix
**Rows 64–68:** Oat
**Row 69:** Blue Mix
**Rows 70–71:** Rose Pink
**Row 72:** Bright Pink
**Rows 73–108:** Pale Green Mix
**Row 109:** Bracken
**Rows 110–111:** Rose Pink
**Rows 112–116:** Purple Heather
**Rows 117–119:** Bracken
**Rows 120–123:** Pale Lilac
**Row 124:** Bracken
**Rows 125–127:** Teal
**Rows 128–130:** Bracken
**Row 131:** Teal
**Row 132:** Blue Mix
**Row 133:** Oat
**Row 134:** Blue Mix
**Row 135:** Oat
**Rows 136–137:** Pale Lilac
**Row 138:** Blue Mix
**Rows 139–141:** Rose Mix

**Row 142:** Blue Mix
**Rows 143–144:** Pale Lilac
**Row 145:** Teal
**Row 146:** Oat
**Rows 147–148:** Bracken
**Rows 149–151:** Blue Mix
**Rows 152–155:** Teal
**Row 156:** Bracken
**Rows 157–160:** Pale Lilac
**Rows 161–163:** Bracken
**Rows 164–168:** Purple Heather
**Rows 169–170:** Pale Lilac
**Row 171–172:** Rose Pink
**Row 173:** Bracken
**Rows 174–186:** Pale Green Mix
Repeat stripe sequence of 186 rows 4 times (scarf measures approximately 93in/236cm)
Cast off.

## Finishing

Tidy loose ends back into own colours. Press scarf heavily to obtain correct width. Make 14 x 1½in (3cm) diameter pompoms. Two each with C, F, E, G and B and 4 with D. Attach to both ends of scarf using picture as guide.

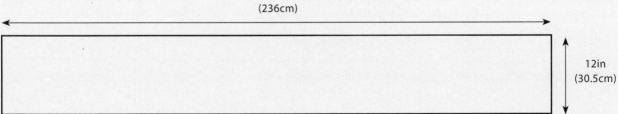

93in
(236cm)

12in
(30.5cm)

This retro 1940s-style short-sleeved sweater looks nostalgically at post-war frugal fashion as worn by my mother. Today's interest in vintage design ensures a revival of this elegant and timeless look.

# Dotty short-sleeved sweater

## Sizes
XS[S:M:L:XL]
**To fit bust**
34[36:38:40:42]in (86[91:96:101:106]cm)
**Actual measurements**
34[36:38:40:42]in (86[91:96:101:106]cm)
**Length**
18½[19:19:19½:19½]in
(47[48.25:48.25:49.5:49.5]cm)
**Sleeve seam**
4¾[4¾:4¾:5:5]in
(12[12:12:12.75:12.75]cm)
*Figures in square brackets refer to larger sizes; where there is only one set of figures this applies to all sizes.*

## You will need
Jamieson & Smith Shetland wool
2-ply jumper weight (knits as 4-ply)
(129yds/118m per 25g ball)
6[7:7:8:8] balls 203 **Silver Grey (A)**
3[3:3:4:4] balls 1A **Ivory (B)**
1[1:2:2:2] balls 121 **Mustard (C)**
1 ball FC38 **Bracken (D)**
1 ball FC12 **Olive Mix (E)**
1 ball 49 **Lilac (F)**
1 ball 101 **Rose (G)**
1 ball FC14 **Bressay Blue (H)**
1 pair each 2.75mm (US2:UK12) and
3.25mm (US3:UK10) needles
2.75mm (US2:UK12) circular needle
Stitch holder
Button

## Tension
28 sts and 30 rows to 4in (10cm)
over chart pattern.
*Use larger or smaller needles if necessary to obtain correct tension.*

## Pattern notes
This design uses 2-colour stranded knitting, see page 154.
Mock cable rib pattern
**Row 1:** *P1, k into 2nd stitch, then into 1st stitch, slide both stitches off tog; rep from * to last st, p1.
**Row 2:** K1, *p2, k1; rep from * to end of row.

## Back

Using 2.75mm needles and A, cast on 119[127:135:141:149] sts. Work 3½in (9cm) in mock cable rib, ending on WS row and dec 1 st on this row (118[126:134:140:148] sts). Change to 3.25mm needles and refer to chart and work the 78 rows, then rows 1–10 (88 rows), centring as foll: Work last 5[3:1:4:2] sts, work the 12 sts of chart 9[10:11:11:12] times across row, work first 5[3:1:4:2] sts (118[126:134:140:148] sts). Cont in patt as set until work measures 11½[11¾:11½:11¾:11½] in (29.25[30:29.25:30:29.25]cm) from cast-on edge ending on WS row.

### Shape armholes

Cast off 6[7:7:8:8] sts at beg of next 2 rows, keeping patt correct as set. Then cast off a further 2[2:3:3:4] sts at beg of next 6 rows. Then dec 1 st at both ends of next and every alternate row 8[10:10:11:11] times (78[80:82:84:86] sts). Cont straight in patt until all 88 chart rows are completed.

**Next row:** Using B, k across row.
**Next row:** Using A, p across row, inc 1 st at end (79[81, 83, 85, 87] sts). *
Cont in A and mock cable rib to end. When work measures 16½[17:17:17½:17½] in (42[43:43:44.5:44.5]cm) from cast-on edge ending on WS row, make slit.

### Divide for yoke slit

Patt 39[40:41:42:43] sts and turn, place rem sts on a holder. Cont in patt on these sts for right back neck until work measures 17¾[18¼:18¼:18¾:18¾]in (45[46.5:46.5:47.75:47.75]cm) from cast-on edge ending on WS row.

### Shape shoulder

**Next row:** Patt 15[15:15:16:17] sts and turn, place rem 24[25:26:26:26] sts on a stitch holder.

**Next Row:** Patt to end.
Cast off 5 sts at beg of next row. Work 1 row. Cast off 5[5:5:5:6] sts at beg of foll row. Work 1 row. Cast off rem 5[5:5:6:6] sts.
Rejoin yarn to rem 40[41:42:43:44] sts. Work left back neck to match right back neck reversing all shapings, leaving 25[26:27:27:27] sts on holder.

## Front

Work as for back to *.
Cont in mock cable patt and A until work measures 15½[16:16:16½:16½]in (39.5[40.75:40.75:42:42]cm) from cast-on edge ending on WS row.

### Shape neck

Patt 29[30:31:32:33] sts and turn. Place rem sts on a stitch holder. Dec 1 st at neck edge on next and every row 14[15:16:16:16] times. Work in patt until work measures 17¾[18¼:18¼:18¾:18¾]in (45[46.5:46.5:47.75:47.75]cm) from cast-on edge ending on WS row.

### Shape shoulder

Cast off 5 sts at beg of next row. Work 1 row. Cast off 5[5:5:5:6] sts at beg of foll row. Work 1 row. Cast off rem 5[5:5:6:6] sts.
Slip 21 sts onto stitch holder for centre front, rejoin yarn to rem sts. Work right side of neck to match left reversing shaping.

## Sleeves

Using 2.75mm needles and A cast on 91[91:94:97:97] sts. Work 1in(2.5cm) in mock cable rib ending on WS row. Change to 3.25mm needles and refer to chart and work to end, starting on chart row 31[33:31:31:29]. Then work chart rows 1–44[46:46:46:46] (92[92:94:94:96] rows in all). Centre chart as foll: Work last 3[3:5:0:0] sts, work the 12 sts of chart 7[7:7:8:8] times, work first 4[4:5:1:1] sts.
At the same time inc as foll:
**XS:** 1 st at both ends of 11th and foll 10th row keeping patt correct (95 sts).
**S and M:** 1 st at both ends of 3rd, then ev foll 6th row 3 times, keeping patt correct (99[102] sts).
**L:** 1 st at both ends of 5th, then ev foll 4th row 4 times, keeping patt correct (107 sts).
**XL:** 1 st at both ends of the next, then every alt row twice, then every 4th row 4 times, keeping patt correct (111 sts).
Work in patt as set until sleeve measures 4¾[4¾:4¾:5:5]in (12[12:12:12.75:12.75]cm) from cast-on edge ending on WS row.

### Shape sleeve cap

Cast off 6[7:7:8:8] sts at beg of next 2 rows, keeping patt correct as set.
**Dec as foll:**
**XS:** Dec 1 st at both ends of next, then every alt row 5 times, then every 4th row 8 times (67sts).
**S:** Dec 1 st at both ends of next, then every alt row 8 times, then every 4th row 7 times (67sts).
**M:** Dec 1 st at both ends of next, then every alt row 10 times, then every 4th row 6 times (68 sts).
**L:** Dec 1 st at both ends of next, then every alt row 16 times, then every 4th row 3 times (67 sts).

**XL:** Dec 1 st at both ends of next, then every alt row 21 times (67 sts).
**For M only:** Dec 1 st at beg of next row. Cont in patt as set until chart row 40[42:42:42:42] is completed – 88[88:90:90:92] rows of chart patt. Cast off 2 sts at beg of next 4 rows (59 sts).
**Next row:** Using A, k3tog across row to last 2 sts, k2tog.
Cast off rem 20 sts tightly.

## Neckband

Join shoulder seams.
Using 2.75mm circular needle, with RS facing and A and starting at left side of back neck, place 24[25:26:26:26] sts from stitch holder onto the needle.
Pick up and k 39[39:40:40:40] sts down left neck, rib 21 sts from centre front holder, pick up 39[39:40:40:40] sts up right neck, rib 25[26:27:27:27] sts from holder at right back neck (148[148:154:154:154] sts).
Taking care to keep ribbing in line, work row 2 of mock cable rib across all sts.
Cont in mock cable rib until neckband measures 1in (2.5cm), ending on WS row. Cast off in rib, leaving enough yarn to make a loop.

## Finishing

Tidy loose ends back into own colours. Press pieces lightly on WS avoiding ribbing. Sew side and sleeve seams in one line. Sew sleeve into armhole, placing fullness evenly across shoulder and matching Fair Isle patterns. Sew button at top of left back neck opening. Make button loop at top of right back neck opening. Steam seams.

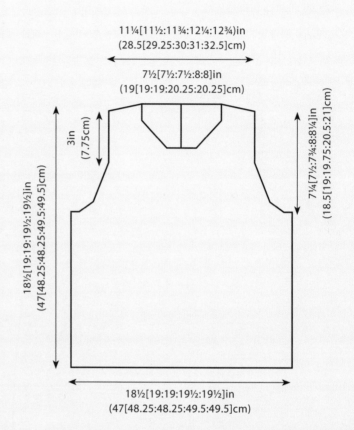

11¼[11½:11¾:12¼:12¾]in
(28.5[29.25:30:31:32.5]cm)

7½[7½:7½:8:8]in
(19[19:19:20.25:20.25]cm)

3in
(7.75cm)

7¼[7½:7¾:8:8¼]in
(18.5[19:19.75:20.5:21]cm)

18½[19:19:19½:19½]in
(47[48.25:48.25:49.5:49.5]cm)

18½[19:19:19½:19½]in
(47[48.25:48.25:49.5:49.5]cm)

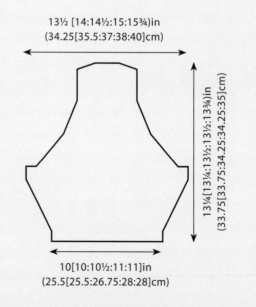

13½ [14:14½:15:15¾]in
(34.25[35.5:37:38:40]cm)

13¼[13¼:13½:13½:13¾]in
(33.75[33.75:34.25:34.25:35]cm)

10[10:10½:11:11]in
(25.5[25.5:26.75:28:28]cm)

# Dotty chart (12 sts x 78 rows)

## Key to chart

- **A** Silver Grey
- **B** Ivory
- **C** Mustard
- **D** Bracken
- **E** Olive Mix
- **F** Lilac
- **G** Rose
- **H** Bressay Blue

*1 square represents one stitch and one row*

**12 sts**

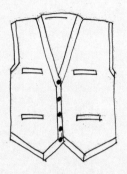

An early foray into the joy of
interlocking shapes. First seen
in Covent Garden's Scottish
Merchant shop, London, these
waistcoats were destined for
Cagney and Lacy to wear in the
famous 1970s TV series.

# Spot tuxedo waistcoat

## Sizes
XS[S:M:L:XL]
**To fit bust**
34[36:38:40:42]in
(86[91:96:101:106]cm)
**Actual measurements**
36[38:40:42:44]in
(91[96:101:106:111]cm)
**Length**
23[23:23:24:24]in (58[58:58:61:61]cm)
*Figures in square brackets refer to larger
sizes; where there is only one set of
figures this applies to all sizes.*

## You will need
Jamieson & Smith Shetland wool
2-ply jumper weight (knits as 4-ply)
(129yds/118m per 25g ball)
6[7:7:7:7] balls 36 **Navy (A)**
1 ball FC38 **Bracken (B)**
1 ball FC9 **Lilac Mix (C)**
1 ball 203 **Silver Grey (D)**
1 ball FC12 **Olive Mix (E)**
1 ball 78 **Dark Fawn (F)**
1 ball FC24 **Moss Green FC24 (G)**
1 pair each 2.75mm (US2:UK12),
3mm (US3:UK11) and 3.25mm
(US4:UK10) needles
5 x ½in (1cm) buttons

## Tension
27 sts and 34 rows to 4in (10cm)
over chart pattern.
37 sts and 36 rows to 4in (10cm)
over twisted rib pattern.
*Use larger or smaller needles
if necessary to obtain correct tension.*

## Pattern notes
This design uses 2-colour stranded
knitting, see page 154.

## Back

Using 2.75mm needles and A cast on 122[130:140:150:158] sts
Work in k1, p1 twisted rib, at the same time inc 1 st at both ends of 8th, then every foll 6th row until there are 144[152:162:172:180] sts, keeping rib correct.
Cont without shaping until the work measures 9[9:9:9½:9½]in (23[23:23:24:24]cm) from cast-on edge.

### Shape armholes

Cast off 9[10:10:11:11] sts at beg of next 2 rows. Then dec 1 st at both ends of next and ev alt row until 110[112:116:118:120] sts remain. Cont without further shaping until work measures 17¾[17¾:17¾:18¾:18¾]in (45[45:45:47.5:47.5]cm).

### Shape shoulders

Cast off 12 sts at beg of next 4 rows.
Cast off 12[13:13:13:13] sts at beg of next 2 rows.
Cast off rem 38[38:42:44:46] sts.

## Right front

Using 3.25mm needles and A cast on 2 sts. Refer to chart and repeat the 42 rows to end. Start chart on sts 1 and 2, adding more of chart at beg and end as you increase.

### XS

**Row 1:** K twice into first st, k1.
**Row 2:** P3.
**Row 3:** Knit, increasing 1 st in first st and last st (5 sts).
**Row 4:** Cast on 2 sts, p to last 2 sts, inc in next st, p1 (8 sts).
**Rows 5–14:** Repeat rows 3 and 4 five times (33 sts).
**Row 15:** K, increasing 1 st in first st and last st (35 sts).
**Row 16:** Cast on 2 sts, p to end (37 sts).
**Rows 17–28:** Repeat rows 15 and 16 six times (61 sts).
**Row 29:** K across row.
**Row 30:** Cast on 2 sts, p to end (63 sts).

### S

**Row 1:** K twice into first st, k1.
**Row 2:** P3.
**Row 3:** K, increasing 1 st in first st and last st (5 sts).
**Row 4:** Cast on 3 sts, p to last 2 sts, inc in next st, p1 (9 sts).
**Rows 5–10:** Repeat rows 3 and 4 three times (27 sts).
**Row 11:** K, increasing 1 st in first st and last st (29 sts).
**Row 12:** Cast on 2 sts, p to end (31 sts).
**Rows 13–30:** Repeat rows 11 and 12 nine times (67 sts).

### M

**Row 1:** K twice into first st, k1.
**Row 2:** P3.
**Row 3:** K, increasing 1 st in first st and last st (5 sts).
**Row 4:** Cast on 3 sts, p to last 2 sts, inc in next st, p1 (9 sts).
**Rows 5–14:** Repeat rows 3 and 4 five times (39 sts).
**Row 15:** K, increasing 1 st in first st and last st (41 sts).
**Row 16:** Cast on 2 sts, p to end (43 sts).
**Rows 17–30:** Repeat rows 15 and 16 seven times (71 sts).

### L

**Row 1:** K twice into first st, k1.
**Row 2:** P3.
**Row 3:** K, increasing 1 st in first st and last st (5 sts).
**Row 4:** Cast on 3 sts, p to last 2 sts, inc in next st, p1 (9 sts).
**Rows 5–16:** Repeat rows 3 and 4 six times (45 sts).
**Row 17:** K, increasing 1 st in first st and last st (47 sts).
**Row 18:** Cast on 2 sts, p to end (49 sts).
**Rows 19–30:** Repeat rows 15 and 16 six times (73 sts).

### XL

**Row 1:** K twice into first st, k1.
**Row 2:** P3.
**Row 3:** K, increasing 1 st in first st and last st (5 sts).

**Row 4:** Cast on 3 sts, p to last 2 sts, inc in next st, p1 (9 sts).
**Rows 5–20:** Repeat rows 3 and 4 eight times (57 sts).
**Row 21:** K, increasing 1 st in first st and last st (59 sts).
**Row 22:** Cast on 2 sts, p to end (61 sts).
**Rows 23–30:** Repeat rows 21 and 22 four times (77 sts).
Work in patt for 3in (7.5cm) ending on WS row.

### Work pocket

**Next row:** K18[20:22:23:25] sts, cast off 27 sts, k to end.
**Next row:** P18[20:22:23:25] sts, cast on 27 sts, p to end.
Cont in patt, inc 1 st at end of first row (RS) and then again on 22nd row after pocket rows – 65[69:73:75:79] sts. Cont in patt until straight edge at centre front measures 7[7:7:8:8]in (17.75[17.75:17.75:20.5:20.5]cm) ending on WS row.

### Shape front neck edge

Dec 1 st at neck edge on next and every 5th row 14[14:15:16:17] times. At the same time work armholes when work measures 8[8:8:8½:8½]in (20.5[20.5:20.5:21.5:21.5]cm) along side edge, ending on RS row.

### Shape armholes

Cast off 6[7:7:8:8] sts, p to end.
Work 1 row then dec 1 st at beg of next and every foll alt row 19[21:24:24:27] times.
At the same time when work measures 8½[8½:8½:9:9]in (21.5[21.5:21.5:23:23]cm) along side edge, ending on WS row, work pocket as before, placing it directly above the lower pocket.
Cont in patt until work measures 16¾[16¾:16¾:17¾:17¾:]in (42.5[42.5:42.5:45:45]cm) ending on RS row.

## Shape shoulder

Cast off 8[9:9:9:9] sts at beg of next row. Work 1 row.
Cast off 9 sts at beg of next and foll alt row.

## Left front

Using 3.25mm needles and A cast on 2 sts. Refer to chart and repeat the 42 rows to end. Start chart on sts 1 and 2, adding more of chart at beg and end as you increase. Work as for right front reversing all shapings and pocket placements. Work shaping at bottom of front as foll:

### XS

**Row 1:** K twice into first st, k1.
**Row 2:** P3.
**Row 3:** K, increasing 1 st in first st and last st (5 sts).
**Row 4:** P1, inc in next st, p to end, cast on 2 sts (8 sts).
**Rows 5–14:** Repeat rows 3 and 4 five times (33 sts).
**Row 15:** K, increasing 1 st in first st and last st (35 sts).
**Row 16:** P to end, cast on 2 sts (37 sts).
**Rows 17–28:** Repeat rows 15 and 16 six times (61 sts).
**Row 29:** K across row.
**Row 30:** P to end, cast on 2 sts (63 sts).

### S

**Row 1:** K twice into first st, k1.
**Row 2:** P3.
**Row 3:** K, increasing 1 st in first st and last st (5 sts).
**Row 4:** P1, inc in next st, p to end, cast on 3 sts (9 sts).
**Rows 5–10:** Repeat rows 3 and 4 three times (27 sts).
**Row 11:** K, increasing 1 st in first st and last st (29 sts).
**Row 12:** P to end, cast on 2 sts (31 sts).
**Rows 13–30:** Repeat rows 11 and 12 nine times (67 sts).

### M

**Row 1:** K twice into first st, k1.
**Row 2:** P3.
**Row 3:** K, increasing 1 st in first st and last st (5 sts).
**Row 4:** P1, inc 1 st in next st, p to end, cast on 3 sts (9 sts).
**Rows 5–14:** Repeat rows 3 and 4 five times (39 sts).
**Row 15:** K, increasing 1 st in first st and last st (41 sts).
**Row 16:** P to end, cast on 2 sts (43 sts).
**Rows 17–30:** Repeat rows 15 and 16 seven times (71 sts).

### L

**Row 1:** K twice into first st, k1.
**Row 2:** P3.
**Row 3:** K, increasing 1 st in first st and last st (5 sts).
**Row 4:** P1, inc 1 st in next st, p to end, cast on 3 sts (9 sts).
**Rows 5–16:** Repeat rows 3 and 4 six times (45 sts).
**Row 17:** K, increasing 1 st in first st and last st (47 sts).
**Row 18:** P to end, cast on 2 sts (49 sts).
**Rows 19–30:** Repeat rows 15 and 16 six times (73 sts).

### XL

**Row 1:** K twice into first st, k1.
**Row 2:** P3.
**Row 3:** K, increasing 1 st in first st and last st (5 sts).
**Row 4:** P1, inc 1 st in next st, p to end, cast on 3 sts (9 sts).
**Rows 5–20:** Repeat rows 3 and 4 eight times (57 sts).
**Row 21:** K, increasing 1 st in first st and last st (59 sts).
**Row 22:** P to end, cast on 2 sts (61 sts).
**Rows 23–30:** Repeat rows 21 and 22 four times (77 sts).

## Finishing

Join shoulder seams.

### Front borders

Using 2.75mm needles and A cast on 2 sts.
Work k1, p1 twisted rib casting on 2 sts at beg of every alt row until 12 sts are on the needle.
Cont until start of straight front edge on right front.
**Next row:** Rib 4, cast off 3 sts for buttonhole, rib 5.
**Next row:** Rib 5, cast on 3 sts, rib 4.
Mark the position of 4 more buttonholes on right front – one at position where neckline shaping starts and the other three placed evenly between. Cont in rib making 4 more buttonholes at markers, and then cont until border will travel up right side of neck around and down other side, ending at corner of peak.
*NB: border should fit snugly when stretched slightly.*
Starting at the same edge as where the shaping at beg finished, cast off 2 sts at beg of next and every alt row until 2 sts remain. Cast off.

### Lower-edge border (make 2)

Using 2.75mm needles and A, cast on 2 sts.
Work in k1 p1 twisted rib casting on 2 sts at beg of every alt row until there are 12 sts.
Continue in rib until border fits, when stretched slightly, from front point to side seam. Cast off.

### Armhole borders

Using 2.75mm needles, with RS facing and A, pick up and k1 st for each row on front armhole up to shoulder, then the same number of sts evenly spread down back armhole. Work 6 rows in k1 p1 twisted rib. Cast off in rib.

### Pocket borders

Using 2.75mm needles, with RS facing and A, pick up and k26 sts from bottom edges of pocket slits. Work 6 rows in k1, p1 twisted rib. Cast off in rib.

### Pocket linings

Using 3mm needles, with RS facing and A, pick up and k sts across top of pocket slits. Work 2½in (6 cm) in st st. Cast off.

Tidy loose ends back into own colours. Press pieces lightly on WS avoiding ribbing. Sew down the edges of pocket borders and linings. Join lower edge borders to front borders and V points. Pin and sew front borders. Join side seams, making sure lower edge of border is sewn to back at base. Attach buttons opposite buttonholes.

# Spot chart (12 sts x 42 rows)

## Key to chart

- ■ **A** Navy
- ■ **B** Bracken
- ■ **C** Lilac Mix
- □ **D** Silver Grey
- ■ **E** Olive Mix
- ■ **F** Dark Fawn
- ■ **G** Moss Green

*1 square represents one stitch and one row*

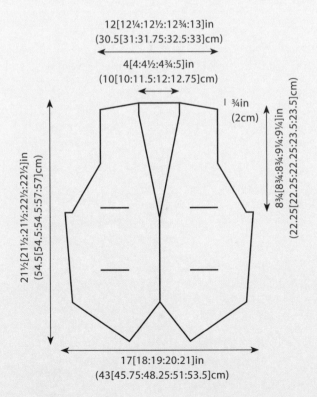

12[12¼:12½:12¾:13]in
(30.5[31:31.75:32.5:33]cm)

4[4:4½:4¾:5]in
(10[10:11.5:12:12.75]cm)

¾in
(2cm)

8¾[8¾:8¾:9¼:9¼]in
(22.25[22.25:22.25:23.5:23.5]cm)

21½[21½:21½:22½:22½]in
(54.5[54.5:54.5:57:57]cm)

17[18:19:20:21]in
(43[45.75:48.25:51:53.5]cm)

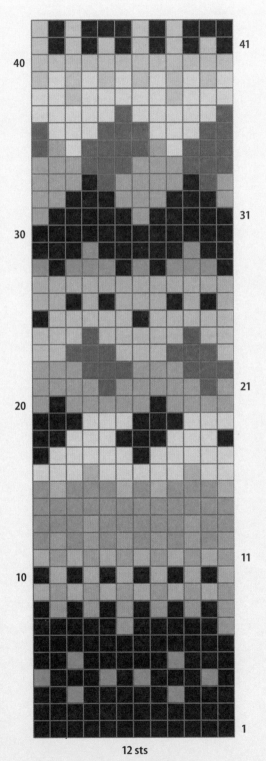

40

41

30

31

20

21

10

11

1

12 sts

David Wade's book *Pattern in Islamic Art*, 1976, influenced my exploration into geometric patterns. I try to achieve balance and harmony in my designs and believe that the feeling will be reflected in the wearer.

# Mosaic V-neck slipover

## Sizes
XS[S:M:L:XL]
**To fit bust**
34[36:38:40:42]in
(86[91:96:101:106]cm)
**Actual measurements**
34[36:38:40:42]in
(86[91:96:101:106]cm)
**Length**
24½[24½:25:25:25½]in
(62[62:63.5:63.5:64.75]cm)
*Figures in square brackets refer to larger sizes; where there is only one set of figures this applies to all sizes.*

## You will need
Jamieson & Smith Shetland wool
2-ply jumper weight (knits as 4-ply)
(129yds/118m per 25g ball)
4[5:5:5:5] balls 36 **Navy (A)**
3[3:3:3:3] balls FC38 **Bracken (B)**
2[2:3:3:3] balls FC12 **Olive (C)**
1[1:2:2:2] ball 82 **Bottle Green (D)**
1[1:1:1:1] ball 1A **Ivory (E)**
1[1:1:1:1] ball 121 **Mustard (F)**
1[1:1:1:1] ball 78 **Dark Fawn (G)**
1[1:1:1:1] ball FC24 **Sage Green (H)**
1[1:1:1:1] ball FC55 **Red Mix (I)**
1 pair each of 2.25mm (US1:UK13),
3mm (US2:UK11) and 3.25mm
(US3:UK10) needles
A set of 4 double-pointed needles size
2.75mm (US2:UK12)
Stitch holder, 2 stitch markers

## Tension
30 sts and 30 rows to 4in (10cm)
over chart pattern.
40 sts and 36 rows to 4in (10cm)
over twisted rib pattern.
*Use larger or smaller needles
if necessary to obtain correct tension.*

## Pattern notes
This design uses 2-colour stranded
knitting, see page 154.

## Back

Using 2.25mm needles and A cast on 150[160:170:180:190] sts.
Work 2in (5cm) k1, p1 twisted rib.
Change to 3mm needles and continue to work back in k1, p1 twisted rib in the following three-colour stripe sequence.
**Row 1:** B.
**Row 2:** C.
**Row 3:** A.
Carry yarns not in use up sides of the work. Cont without shaping until back measures 14½[14½:15:15:15½] in (37[37:38:38:39.5]cm) from cast-on edge ending on a WS row. **
### Shape armholes
Cont in patt cast off 9[10:10:11:11] sts at beg of next 2 rows, then dec 1 st at each end of every alt row until 104[106:110:112:116] sts remain.
Work straight in patt until armhole measures 9¼in (23.5cm) ending on a WS row.
### Shape shoulders
**XS:** Cast off 9 sts at beg of next 2 rows, then 10 sts at beg of foll 4 rows.
**S:** Cast off 10 sts at beg of next 6 rows.
**M:** Cast off 10 sts at beg of next 4 rows, then 11 sts at beg of foll 2 rows.
**L:** Cast off 10 sts at beg of next 2 rows, then 11 sts at beg of foll 4 rows.
**XL:** Cast off 11 sts at beg of next 6 rows.
Place rem 46[46:48:48:50] sts on a holder.

## Front

Using 2.25mm needles and A cast on 134[142:150:158:164] sts.
Work 2in (5cm) in k1, p1 twisted rib, inc 8 sts evenly across the last WS row (142[150:158:166:172] sts).
Change to 3.25mm needles and refer to chart and repeat the 50 rows to end of work.

Centre chart as foll:
**RS rows:** Work the last 3[7:3:7:2] sts of chart, work the 16 sts 8[8:9:9:10] times across row, work the first 3[7:3:7:2] sts of chart (142[150:158:166:172] sts).
**WS rows:** As above but working from left to right.
Cont in patt until work measures same as back to ** ending with a WS row.
### Shape armholes and neck
Continuing in patt, cast off 7[8:8:9:9] sts at beg of next 2 rows (128[134:142:148:154] sts).
K2tog at beginning of next row, work next 61[64:68:71:74] sts and turn, placing next 2 sts on pin and rem 63[66:70:73:76] sts on a holder.
Work back across these 61[64:68:71:74] sts in patt.
Dec 1 st at beg of next and ev alt row 18[20:21:23:25] times.
At the same time, work neck by dec 1 st at neck edge every alt row 16[16:20:20:20] times, then every foll 4th row 4[4:2:2:2] times.
Cont straight in patt on rem 23[24:25:26:27] sts until armhole measures 9¼in (23.5cm) ending on a WS row.
### Shape shoulder
**XS:** Cast off 7 sts at beg of next row, then 8 sts at beg of foll 2 alt rows.
**S:** Cast off 8 sts at beg of next row, then 8 sts at beg of foll 2 alt rows.
**M:** Cast off 8 sts at beg of next and foll alt row, then 9 sts at beg of foll alt row.
**L:** Cast off 8 sts at beg of next row, then 9 sts at beg of foll 2 alt rows.
**XL:** Cast off 9 sts at beg of next row, then 9 sts at beg of foll 2 alt rows.
Work other side to match left shoulder reversing all shapings.

## Neckband

Join right shoulder seam.
Using 2.75mm needles and A and with RS facing begin at left shoulder and pick up and k74 sts down left side of neck to pin, place marker, then pick up and k2 sts from pin at centre front, place another marker, then pick up and k74 sts up right side of neck and the 46[46:48:48:50] sts from holder at centre back neck (196[196:198:198:200] sts).
Work neckband in k1, p1 twisted rib, dec at each side of the 2 centre front sts as foll:
**Row 1:** Rib around back of neck and down right side of neck to within 2 sts of marker, sl 1, k1, psso, p2, k2tog, rib up L side of neck to end.
**Row 2:** Rib down left side of neck to within 2 sts of marker, sl 1, k1, psso, k2, k2tog, rib to end.
Rep rows 1 and 2 four times then work row 1 again.
Join in B and work one row rib as for row 2.
Cast off in rib in B.

## Armbands

Join left shoulder seam and neckband.
Using 2.75mm needles and A pick up and k178 sts around armhole. Work 9 rows k1, p1 twisted rib. Join in B and work 1 row rib. Cast off in rib in B.

## Finishing

Tidy loose ends back into own colours. Press front lightly on WS avoiding ribbing. Join side seams, armbands. Steam seams.

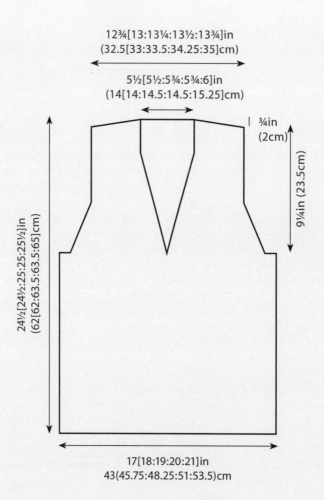

12¾[13:13¼:13½:13¾]in
(32.5[33:33.5:34.25:35]cm)

5½[5½:5¾:5¾:6]in
(14[14:14.5:14.5:15.25]cm)

¾in
(2cm)

9¼in (23.5cm)

24½[24½:25:25:25½]in
(62[62:63.5:63.5:65]cm)

17[18:19:20:21]in
43(45.75:48.25:51:53.5)cm

## Mosaic chart (16 sts x 50 rows)

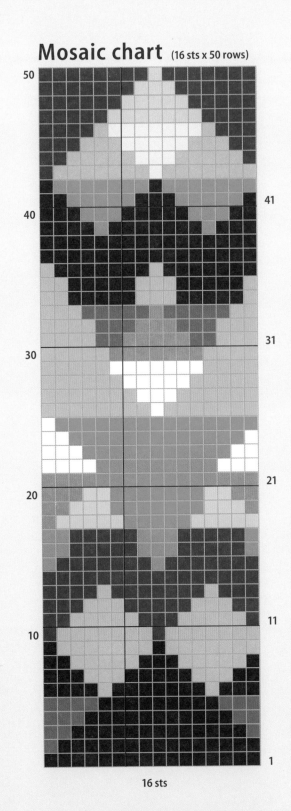

## Key to chart

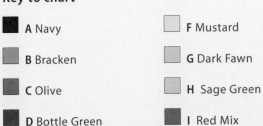

**A** Navy

**B** Bracken

**C** Olive

**D** Bottle Green

**E** Ivory

**F** Mustard

**G** Dark Fawn

**H** Sage Green

**I** Red Mix

*1 square represents one stitch and one row*

**16 sts**

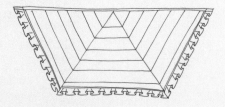

A folkloric influence can be seen in this pretty design. Graphic cherry motifs are used to soften the line between backgrounds, making this new twist on a traditional peasant shawl into a modern classic.

# Cherry shawl

## Sizes
One size fits all
**Actual measurements**
**Width:** 62in (155cm) including ruffle
**Length:** 25in (63.5cm) including ruffle

## You will need
Rowan Cashsoft 4-ply
(175yds/160m per 50g ball)
3 balls 433 **Cream (A)**
1 ball 456 **Aran (B)**
1 ball 438 **Poppy (C)**
Rowan Felted Tweed
(191yds/175m per 50g ball)
5 balls 165 **Scree (D)**
1 ball 150 **Rage (E)**
1 ball 152 **Watery (F)**
1 pair each of 2.75mm (US2:UK12)
and 3.25mm (US3:UK10) needles
1 long 2.75mm (US2:UK12) circular
needle

## Tension
26 sts and 35 rows to 4in (10cm) over chart patt using 3.25mm needles. Change needles if necessary to obtain correct tension.

## Pattern notes
This design uses the intarsia woven method, see page 155.

## Ruffle

**Row 1(RS):** P7, *k1, p7; rep from * to end.

**Row 2:** K7, *p1, k7; rep from * to end.

**Row 3:** P7, *yo, k1, yfrn, p7; rep from * to end.

**Row 4:** K7, *p2, p1 tbl, k7; rep from * to end.

**Row 5:** P7, *yo, k3, yfrn, p7; rem from * to end.

**Row 6:** K7, *p4, p1 tbl, k7; rep from * to end.

**Row 7:** P7, *yo, k5, yfrn, p7; rep from * to end.

**Row 8:** K7, *p6, p1 tbl, k7; rep from * to end.

**Row 9:** P7, *yo, k7, yfrn, p7; rep from * to end.

**Row 10:** K7, *p8, p1 tbl, k7; rep from * to end.

**Row 11:** P7, *yo, k9, yfrn, p7; rep from * to end.

**Row 12:** K7, *p10, p1 tbl, k7; rep from * to end.

**Row 13:** P7, *yo, k11, yfrn, p7; rep from * to end.

**Row 14:** K7, *p12, p1 tbl, k7; rep from * to end.

**Row 15:** P7, *yo, k13, yfrn, p7; rep from * to end.

**Row 16:** K7, *p14, p1 tbl, k7; rep from * to end.

### Picot edge cast off

Cast off 2 sts, *sl st back to LH needle, using the cable cast-on method, cast on 3 sts, then cast off 5 sts; rep from * to end.

## Shawl

**Section 1:** Using 2.75mm needles and A cast on 195 sts and work 4 rows garter stitch.
Change to 3.25mm needles and refer to chart and centre as foll:
Work last 8 sts of chart, work 30 sts of chart 6 times across row, work first 7 sts (195 sts).
Work the 60 rows of patt 3 times, dec 1 st at beg and end of every alt row. Then cont with decs in A until 1 st remains. Cut yarn and pull through loop.

**Sections 2 and 3:** As section 1.

## Finishing

Press each piece lightly on WS.
Using a small neat backstitch on edge of work, join the 3 sections to make a half hexagon.

### Top trim

Using 2.75mm needles with right side facing and A, pick up and k 396 sts across top of shawl – approx 1 st for each row. Work 6 rows garter stitch inc 1 st at beg and end of alt rows (402 sts). Cast off.

### Ruffle trim

**Section 1:** Turn shawl upside down and with RS facing, using 2.75mm needles and D, pick up and k 199 sts from cast-on edge. Purl 1 row. Then refer to ruffle patt and work the 16 rows, rep patt across row, inc 1 st at both ends of every alt row (215 sts).
Cast off using picot edge cast-off.
**Sections 2 and 3:** as Section 1.

Tidy loose ends back into own colours. Join ruffle seams together. Pin out ruffle and press.

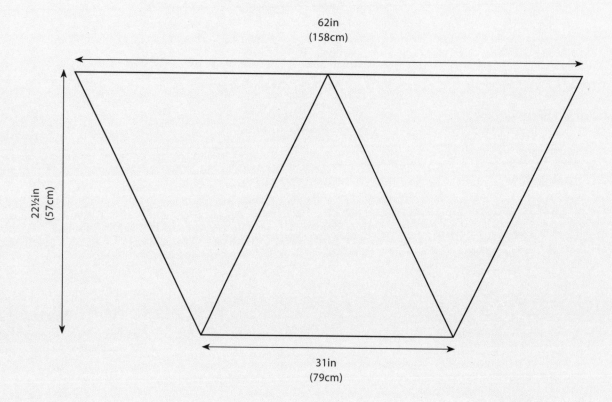

62in
(158cm)

22½in
(57cm)

31in
(79cm)

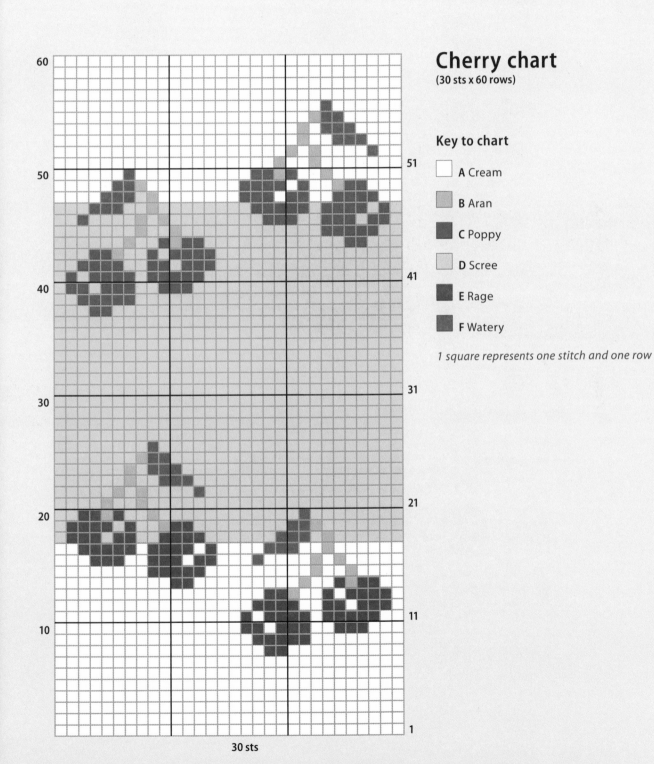

# Cherry chart

**(30 sts x 60 rows)**

## Key to chart

- ☐ **A** Cream
- ▩ **B** Aran
- ▨ **C** Poppy
- ▨ **D** Scree
- ▨ **E** Rage
- ▨ **F** Watery

*1 square represents one stitch and one row*

The birth of the designer knit

# A quiet revolution

**SANDY BLACK**, PROFESSOR OF FASHION AND
TEXTILE DESIGN AND TECHNOLOGY AT THE LONDON
COLLEGE OF FASHION, DESCRIBES HOW FROM
THE EARLY 1970s A NEW WAVE OF DESIGNERS
REDISCOVERED THE DELIGHTS OF HAND KNITTING.

**Above:** A knitting pattern from the 1950s.
**Opposite:** Turkish Carnation Jacket by Kaffe Fassett, 1980.

In contrast to the raucous 1960s 'youthquake' in both music and fashion, pioneered by designers such as Mary Quant, Foale and Tuffin, Barbara Hulaniki of Biba, and Ossie Clark, knitwear remained a largely utilitarian, somewhat staid, element of basic clothing – the commercially mass-produced classics of an older generation. However, during the following decade a quiet revolution in knitwear began. In tandem with a resurgence of interest in handmade crafts and as a backlash to mass production, these designers (mainly self-taught and mainly women) reinterpreted past techniques and joyfully worked with colour and natural materials in a true renaissance of the art.

Despite a wonderfully creative flowering of hand knitting in the austerity years of the 1940s and 1950s, by the 1970s handmade knitwear was considered dowdy and decidedly old-fashioned. As discussed in *Knitwear in Fashion* (Sandy Black, Thames & Hudson, 2002) knitwear was a parallel industry, a Cinderella of fashion, which had arisen out of the important, but essentially practical, hosiery and underwear trade, and which only occasionally intersected with 'real' fashion. In the mid-1960s the advent of miniskirts stimulated a demand for designer stockings and tights, and *Vogue* began to feature new knitted fashions from companies such as the Women's Home Industries, Jaeger and Susan Small.

## 'Knitwear was a Cinderella of fashion, which only occasionally intersected with "real" fashion.'

But it was during the 1970s and early 1980s that a great British burst of creativity occurred, fuelled in part by the strength of its art colleges and higher education in fine arts, textiles and fashion design. The influential fashion writer Suzy Menkes captured the importance of this movement for fashion in her book *The Knitwear Revolution* (Bell and Hyman, 1983), a rare accolade for knitwear to have been dealt with seriously in terms of fashion. My own Vase of Flowers coat design featured on the cover of this book.

Operating quite separately, but responding to the same *Zeitgeist*, individual designers brought their fresh approach to handmade knitwear, focused on colour, texture and often quirky graphic design, inspired by decorative arts of all kinds. Some had studied textiles or fine art, occasionally even fashion, while others were completely self-taught. Whatever the route, a new genre of 'designer knitwear' was born.

**Above:** Front cover of *The Knitwear Revolution* showing Sandy Black's Vase of Flowers coat.

Several key names emerged, each with their own distinctive design repertoire and colourful yarn palettes, including Patricia Roberts, Kaffe Fassett (initially working with Bill Gibb and Missoni and then under his own name), Susan Duckworth, Artwork, Jamie and Jessie Seaton and, of course, Sasha Kagan. As I learnt from personal experience, designer knitwear was initially considered too crafty for serious fashion, and too fashion-orientated for the crafts community. However, designer knitwear quickly found its niche and gained a fantastic following in many countries around the world. Overseas buyers, especially from prestigious department stores in America and Japan (such as Saks Fifth Avenue, Henri Bendel and Bergdorf Goodman in New York) and exclusive boutiques (such as Three Bags Full in Los Angeles and Betsi Bunki Nini in New York), rushed to snap up original knitwear designed in the UK.

Designer knitwear owed its distinctiveness to the fact that the complex, multicoloured and multi-textured designs, using many yarns, could only be made manually (on needles or by manual work on the hand frame) and could not at the time be replicated by mass-production methods. (Only the exceptional Missoni in Italy seemed able to translate its creative vision into colourful machine-made fabrics.) Coupled with this design ethos, the legacy of hand-knitting skills, which had continued to be passed down through many generations, enabled a ready-made work force for these fledgling designer knitwear businesses that rose to the challenge of successfully trading in international markets.

Sasha Kagan's designs exhibit a distinctive handwriting, often inspired by the surrounding Welsh landscape, flowers and the changing seasons. Applying her visual skills, she demonstrates a sure eye for the merging of pattern, scale, colour and texture throughout her many designs, coupled with attention to detail in garment finish and styling. She always aims for 'beauty, style and craftsmanship' and for the last four decades has designed garments that have stood the test of time.

**Above:** The front cover of *Big and Little Sweaters*.

Several themes are regularly revisited, including floral and interlocking geometric patterns in combinations of lusciously coloured natural yarns – the designs scaled to work successfully when on the body. Early signature designs are notable for witty figurative 'nursery' graphics, such as her prowling cats, Scotty dogs and running boys motifs, which although in a simple repeat, flow rhythmically and delight the eye. Strong geometric graphics feature in all the collections and series of five pattern books, but are simpler and more brightly coloured in her second book *Sasha Kagan's Big and Little Sweaters* (Dorling Kindersley, 1987) showing inspiration from the Memphis school. In her more recent compilation *Knitwear* (GMC Publications, 2008), more use is made of stitch structures such as cables and lace, interspersing the floral motifs.

The general public was greatly inspired by designer hand knitting, and the 1980s saw an explosion of designer knitting pattern books, knitting kits and several exhibitions, including The Knitwear Revue (The British Crafts Centre London, 1983), Knit One Purl One (V&A Museum, London, 1985) and Knitting a Common Art (The Minories Colchester and The Crafts Council, touring exhibition, 1986). The first and last in this list featured Sasha Kagan's work alongside designs by myself, Kaffe Fassett, Patricia Roberts, Susan Duckworth, Carrie White, Susie Freeman and several others. In my own exhibition The New Knitting (The Knitting and Stitching Show, London, Harrogate, Dublin, Knutsford, 1998), I included Sasha's Kikan Cape and Pansy sweaters as key pieces in a survey of designer knitwear. Sasha exhibited at the V&A, London, in 2000 to coincide with the publication of *Country Inspiration* (Taunton Press, 2000) and two of her pieces, Annacat ruched sweater and the Hawthorn jacket are in the permanent collections.

Sasha continues to spread her infectious enthusiasm for hand knitting in seminars and workshops worldwide, teaching and writing to encourage new knitters. Even though much has changed technically in the last four decades, with sophisticated technology now available, the depth of colour, detail, richness of texture and personal expression within hand-knitted garments continues to be appreciated. This has great significance in contemporary society, where the mark of the hand and the investment of time in making cannot be mass manufactured.

**Above:** Catalogue from Sasha's 1984 exhibition.

**Left:** Kikan cape, 1977.
**Right:** Prowling Cats design, see page 84 for the pattern.

'THE ERA OF THE DESIGNER KNIT SWEATER –
A RENAISSANCE IN HANDCRAFTS INSPIRED DESIGNERS
FROM ALL DISCIPLINES AND THE KNITWEAR
REVOLUTION WAS BORN.'

1980–89

Scotty has a life of his own as he dances across the decades; snapped up by Henri Bendel and Bergdorf Goodman in the 1970s, he continues to work his charm on today's discerning knitter.

# Scotty dog sweater and beret

## Sizes

**Sweater**
XS[S:M:L:XL]
**To fit bust**
34[36:38:40:42]in (86[91:96:101:106]cm)
**Actual measurements**
36[38:40:42:44]in (91[96:101:106:111]cm)
**Length**
27[27:27:28:28]in
(68.5[68.5:68.5:71.25:71.25]cm)
**Sleeve seam**
18½in (47cm)
**Beret**
To fit average head.
**Actual measurements**
**Width of headband:** 20in (51cm)
**Headband to top:** 9½in (24cm)

*Figures in square brackets refer to larger sizes; where there is only one set of figures this applies to all sizes.*

## You will need

Jamieson & Smith Shetland wool 2-ply jumper weight (knits as 4-ply) (129yds/118m per 25g ball)
**For the sweater:**
10[10:10:11:12] balls 27 **Mid Grey (A)**
3[3:3:4:4] balls 1A **Ivory (B)**
1 ball 1403 **Red (C)**
4[4:4:5:5] balls 77 **Black (D)**
1 ball 65 **Jade (E)**
**For the beret:**
2 balls 27 **Mid Grey (A)**
1 ball 1A **Ivory (B)**
1 ball 1403 **Ruby (C)**
2 balls 77 **Black (D)**

1 ball 65 **Jade (E)**
1 pair each of 2.75mm (US2:UK12) and 3.25mm (US3:UK10) needles.
1 set of 4 double-pointed needles size 2.75mm (US2:UK12)

## Tension

26 sts and 33 rows to 4in (10cm) over chart patt.
*Use larger or smaller needles if necessary to obtain correct tension.*

## Pattern notes

This design uses the intarsia woven method, see page 155.

## Scotty sweater

### Back

Using 2.75mm needles and D cast on 118[124:130:136:144] sts.
Work 2in (5cm) in k1 p1 twisted rib. Change to 3.25mm needles and refer to chart and repeat the 40 rows to end of work.
Centre chart as foll:
**RS rows:** Work the last 9[12:2:5:9] sts of chart, repeat the 25 sts 4[4:5:5:5] times across row, work the first 9[12:3:6:10] sts.
**WS rows:** Work the last 9[12:3:6:10] of chart, repeat the 25 sts 4[4:5:5:5] times across row, work the first 9[12:2:5:9] sts.
Cont in patt until work measures 18[18:18:18½:18½]in (45.75[45.75:45.75:47:47]cm) from cast-on edge, ending on a WS row.
### Shape armholes
Cont in patt, cast off 10[10:10:12:13] sts at beg of next 2 rows ** (98[104:110:112:118] sts).
Work straight in patt until armhole measures 8¼[8¼:8¼:8¾:8¾]in (21[21:21:22.25:22.25]cm) ending on a WS row.
### Shape shoulders
Cast off 10[11:12:12:13] sts at beg of next 6 rows. Place rem 38[38:38:40:40] sts on holder.

### Front

Work as for back to **
98[104:110:112:118] sts.
### Shape neck
With RS facing, work patt across first 49[52:55:56:58] sts, turn; leave rem sts on holder.
**Next row (WS):** K2tog, then leave this st on pin, work to end of row.
Cont patt on these 47[50:53:54:56] sts, dec 1 st at neck edge on next and every alt row 5[5:5:7:7] times in all, then every 4th row 12[12:12:11:11]

times (30[33:36:36:39] sts).
Cont straight until armhole measures 8¼[8¼:8¼:8¾:8¾]in (21[21:21:22.25:22.25]cm) ending on a WS row.
### Shape shoulder
Cast off 10[11:12:12:13] sts at beg of next and every alt row 3 times in all.
With RS facing, rejoin yarn at neck edge to rem 49[52:55:56:58] sts, k2tog and place resulting st on pin, then work in patt to end of row. Work 1 row, then dec right neck edge to match left side.

### Sleeves

Using 2.75mm needles and yarn D cast on 56[56:56:62:62] sts.
Work 3½in (9cm) in k1 p1 twisted rib ending on WS row, inc 6 sts evenly across final row (62[62:62:68:68] sts).
Change to 3.25mm needles and refer to chart and repeat the 40 rows to end of work.
Centre chart as foll:
**RS rows:** Work the last 6[6:6:6:9] sts of chart, repeat the 25 sts twice across row, work the first 6[6:6:6:9] sts.
**WS rows:** Work the last 6[6:6:6:9] sts of chart, repeat the 25 sts twice across row, work the first 6[6:6:6:9] sts.
At the same time inc 1 st at both ends of every 6th row 12 times, then every 4th row 11 times adding extra sts to chart patt as they occur (108[108:108:114:114] sts).
Work straight in patt until sleeve measures 20[20:20:20¼:20¼]in (51[51:51:51.5:52]cm) from cast-on edge, ending on WS row, then cast off loosely.

### Neckband

Use a small neat backstitch on edge of work for all seams except ribs, where a slipstitch should be used.
Join shoulder seams.
With RS facing and using 2.75mm dpns and yarn D, beg at left shoulder seam, pick up and k76 sts down left neck edge, then k1 st from pin at centre front onto 1st needle; on 2nd needle, k1 st from other pin, then pick up and k75sts up right side of neck; on 3rd needle place 38[38:38:40:40] sts on stitch holder at back neck (191[191:191:193:193] sts).
Work 8 rounds k1, p1 twisted rib, dec on every round at centre front as foll:
**1st needle:** Work 74 sts in twisted rib, k2tog, k1.
**2nd needle:** K1, k2tog, starting with a purl st, work 73 sts in twisted rib.
**3rd needle:** Starting with a knit st, work across all sts in twisted rib.
On subsequent rounds keep ribs and decs correct (175[175:175:177:177] sts).
Cast off in rib working 2 sts tog at each side of centre front as set.

### Finishing

Tidy loose ends back into own colours. Press pieces lightly on WS avoiding ribbing. Sew cast off edge of sleeve seam into straight armhole edge. Sew top 1½[1½:1½:1¾:2]in (4[4:4:4.5:5]cm) of sleeve to cast-off edge of armhole forming a neat right-angle. Join side seams and sleeve seams in one line. Steam seams.

## Scotty beret

### Band

Using a pair of 2.75mm needles and D cast on 140 sts.

Work 3in (7.5cm) in k1, p1 twisted rib, then inc as foll:

**Next row (RS):** * K3, m1 (by picking up loop between last and next stitch). Rep from * to end (186 sts).

**Next row (WS):** P inc 14 sts evenly across row (200 sts).

Change to pair of 3.25 mm needles and A and work 2 rows st st, then refer to chart and work the 40 rows. Work a further 2 rows st st with A. Change to set of four 2.75mm needles and distribute sts evenly over three of the needles.

### Shape crown

**Round 1:** Using D and with RS facing *K8, sl 1, k1, psso; rep from * around (180 sts).

**Round 2:** K.

**Round 3:** P.

**Round 4:** *K7, sl 1, k1, psso; rep from * to end (160 sts).

**Round 5:** K.

**Round 6:** K.

**Round 7:** *K6, sl 1, k1, psso; rep from * to end (140 sts).

**Round 8:** P.

Cont thus, working in st st with a purl row every 5th row, dec every 3rd row as foll:

**Round 10:** *K5, sl 1, k1, psso; rep from * to end (120 sts).

**Round 13:** *P4, sl 1, p1, psso; rep from * to end (100 sts).

**Round 16:** *K3, sl 1, k1, psso; rep from * to end (80 sts).

**Round 19:** *K2, sl 1, k1, psso; rep from * to end (60 sts).

**Round 22:** *K1, sl 1, k1, psso; rep from * to end (40 sts).

**Round 23:** P.

**Round 24:** K2tog around (20 sts).

**Round 25:** K2tog around (10 sts).

Break yarn, leaving a 10in (25.5cm) tail and thread through all rem sts.

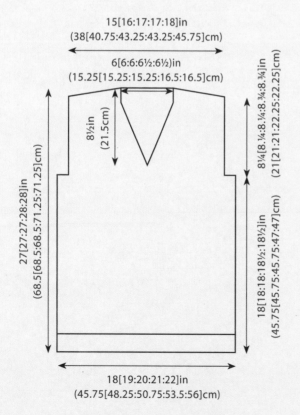

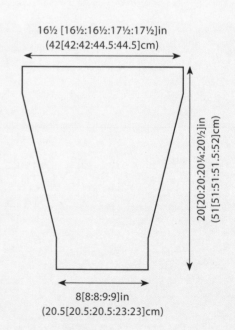

## Stalk

Using pair of 2.75mm needles and C, cast on 14 sts. Cast off.

## Finishing

Fold stalk in half and secure in centre of beret tightening rem sts from centre of beret. Sew up back seam. Fold band to the inside and hem in place. Steam seam and press beret into a circle above white dogs.

# Scotty chart
**(25 sts x 40 rows)**

## Key to chart

 **A** Mid Grey

**B** Ivory

**C** Ruby

**D** Black

**E** Jade

*1 square represents one stitch and one row*

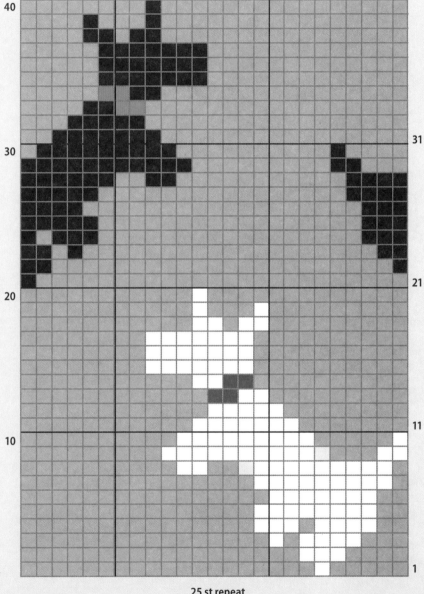

25 st repeat

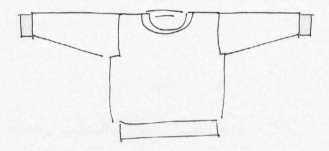

A must for all cat lovers, Staring and Prowling Cats paired well with the Scotty and Dachshund designs. Dubbed 'witty and whimsical', they were first published in *The Sasha Kagan Sweater Book* in 1984.

# Prowling cats sweater

## Sizes
XS[S:M:L:XL]
**To fit bust**
34[36:38:40:42]in (86[91:96:101:106]cm)
**Actual measurements**
38[40:42:44:46]in
(96.5[101.5:106.5:111.75:117]cm)
**Length**
26½[26½:27:27:27½]in
(67.5[67.5:68.5:68.5:70]cm)
**Sleeve seam**
17in (43cm)
*Figures in square brackets refer to larger sizes; where there is only one set of figures this applies to all sizes.*

## You will need
Jamieson & Smith Shetland wool 2-ply jumper weight (knits as 4-ply)
(129yds/118m per 25g ball)
10[10:11:11:12] balls 9113 **Dark Red (A)**
4[5:5:5:6] balls 77 **Black (B)**
5[6:6:6:7] balls 202 **Oat (C)**
1 ball 65 **Jade (D)**
1 ball 121 **Mustard (E)**
Optional 1yd (1m) thin black elastic
1 pair each of 2.75mm (US2:UK12)
and 3.25mm (US3:UK11) needles
Set of 4 double-pointed 2.75mm
(US2:UK12) needles
Stitch holders

## Tension
26 sts and 32 rows to 4in (10cm) over chart patt.
*Use larger or smaller needles if necessary to obtain correct tension.*

## Pattern notes
This design uses the intarsia woven method, see page 155.

## Back

Using 2.75mm needles and B cast on 124[130:136:144:150] sts. Work 21 rows k1, p1 twisted rib in foll stripe sequence:

**Row 1:** B
**Row 2:** A
**Row 3:** A
**Row 4:** B

Change to 3.25mm needles and purl 1 row. Then refer to chart and work 3 repeats. Centre chart as foll:
Work last 2[5:8:12:0] sts, work 30 sts of chart 4[4:4:4:5] times, work first 2[5:8:12:0] sts.
Cont in patt as set until work measures 17¾in (45cm) from cast-on edge ending on a WS row.

### Shape armholes

Cast off 10 sts at beg of next 2 rows. Work straight in patt as set until work measures 25¾[25¾:26¼:26¼:26¾]in (65.5[65.5:66.75:66.75:68]cm) from cast-on edge ending on WS row.
*NB: when 3 reps of chart are completed, work to end in A.*
Cast off 9[10:11:12:13] sts at beg of next 2 rows.
Cast off 10[11:11:13:14] sts at beg of foll 2 rows.
Cast off 10[11:12:13:14] sts at beg of foll 2 rows.
Place rem 46[46:48:48:48] sts on stitch holder.

## Front

Work as for back until work measures 22[22:22½:22½:23]in (56[56:57:57:58.5]cm).

### Shape neck

Work 35[38:40:44:47] sts in patt, leave the foll 34[34:36:36:36] sts on holder, join a second ball of yarn and cont to work next 35[38:40:44:47] sts in patt. Working both sides at the same time in patt as set, dec 1 st at neck edge on the next 6 rows. Cont in patt until work measures 25¾[25¾:26¼:26¼:26¾]in (65.5[65.5:66.75:66.75:68]cm) from cast-on edge ending on WS row (RS row for right neck edge).

### Shape shoulder

Cast off 9[10:11:12:13] sts at beg of next row. Work 1 row.
Cast off 10[11:11:13:14] sts at beg of foll row. Work 1 row.
Cast off rem 10[11:12:13:14] sts.

## Sleeves

Using 2.75mm needles and B cast on 56[56:56:62:62] sts and work 21 rows in k1, p1 twisted rib in stripe sequence as for back, inc 4 sts across final row (60[60:60:66:66] sts).
Change to 3.25mm needles and purl 1 row. Refer to chart and work the 62 rows twice, then work to end in A. Centre chart as foll:
Work the last 0[0:0:3:3] sts, work 30 sts of chart twice, work first 0[0:0:3:3] sts.
At the same time starting on ch row 1, inc 1 st at both ends of first and then every 4th row 8[8:17:8:17] times, then every foll 6th row 13[13:7:13:7] times, keeping chart patt correct (104[104:110:110:116] sts).
Cont in patt as set until sleeve measures 18½in (47cm) from cast-on edge, then cast off.

## Finishing

Join shoulder seams.

### Neckband

Using 4 double-pointed 2.75mm needles, with RS and A join yarn at left shoulder. Pick up and k34 sts down side of neck, 34[34:36:36:36] sts from holder at centre front, 34 sts up right side of neck and 46[46:48:48:48] sts from holder at back neck (148[148:152:152:152] sts).
Work 19 rows in stripe sequence as for back starting at row 2. Cast off in rib with B.
For a close-fitting neck, thread elastic through the last two black stripes. Tidy loose ends back into own colours. Press pieces lightly on WS avoiding ribbing.
Sew cast-off edge of sleeve into straight armhole edge. Sew top 1½in (3.75cm) of sleeve to cast off edge of armhole forming a neat right angle. Join side seams and sleeve seams in one line. Steam seams.

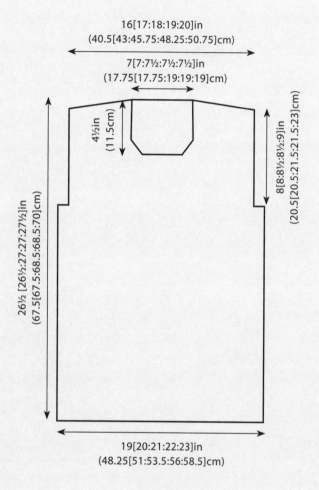

16[17:18:19:20]in
(40.5[43:45.75:48.25:50.75]cm)

7[7:7½:7½:7½]in
(17.75[17.75:19:19:19]cm)

4½in
(11.5cm)

8[8½:8½:8½:9]in
(20.5[20.5:21.5:21.5:23]cm)

26½ [26½:27:27:27½]in
(67.5[67.5:68.5:68.5:70]cm)

19[20:21:22:23]in
(48.25[51:53.5:56:58.5]cm)

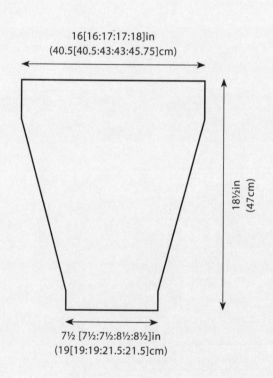

16[16:17:17:18]in
(40.5[40.5:43:43:45.75]cm)

18½in
(47cm)

7½ [7½:7½:8½:8½]in
(19[19:19:21.5:21.5]cm)

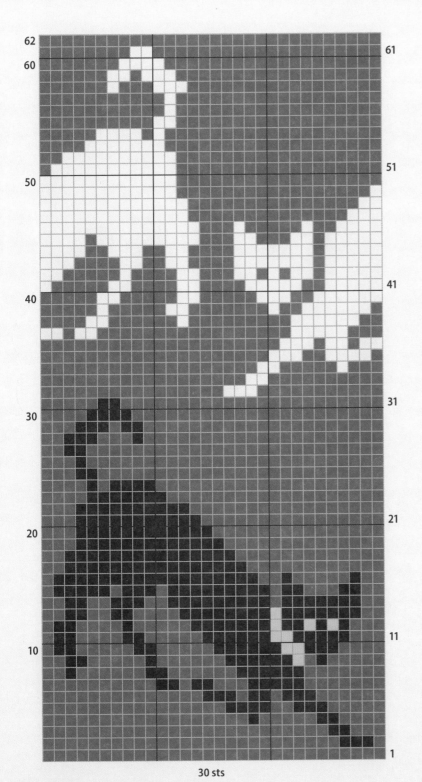

# Prowling cats chart
**(30 sts x 62 rows)**

## Key to chart

**A** Dark Red

**B** Black

**C** Oat

**D** Jade

**E** Mustard

*1 square represents one stitch and one row*

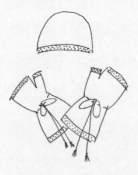

My woven ribbon collection provided the starting point for this folk-inspired flower print. This design can be repeated or used for a border, and was first published in *Big and Little Sweaters* in 1987.

# Bavarian flower beanie & fingerless gloves

## Sizes

**Beanie**
To fit average size head 21in (53cm) circumference.

**Fingerless gloves**
To fit average size hands 7½in (19cm) round width of hand.
**Length**
8½in (21.5cm)

## You will need

Rowan Cashsoft 4-ply
(175yds/160m per 50g ball)
2 balls 422 **Black (A)**
1 ball 438 **Poppy (B)**
1 ball 444 **Amethyst (C)**
Rowan Pure Wool 4-ply
(174 yds/160m per 50g ball)
1 ball 426 **Hyacinth (D)**
1 ball 457 **Quarry Tile (E)**
1 pair each 2.75mm (US2:UK12) and 3.25mm (US3:UK10)
Set of four 2.75mm (US2:UK12) and 3.25mm (US3:UK10) double-pointed needles

## Tension

30 sts and 32 rows to 4in (10cm) over chart patt using 3.25mm needles.
*Change needles if necessary to obtain correct tension.*

## Pattern notes

This design uses 2-colour stranded knitting, see page 154.

## Beanie

Using 2.75mm needles and A, cast on 160 sts, work 8 rows in moss st. Change to 3.25mm needles and refer to chart and repeat the 16 sts 10 times around. Work the 20 rows twice, then cont to end in A.

### Shape crown

**Next round:** *K29, k3tog; rep from * around.

**Next round:** Knit.

**Next round:** *K27, k3tog; rep from * around.

**Next round:** Knit.

**Next round:** *K25, k3tog; rep from * around.

**Next round:** Knit.

Cont dec thus on next round and every foll alt round until 10 sts rem.

**Next round:** *K2tog; rep from * around. Cut yarn, thread through rem sts, pull up and fasten off.

## Fingerless gloves

### Left-hand glove

Using 2.75mm needles and A cast on 80 sts and work 6 rows in moss st. Change to 3.25mm needles and refer to chart and work 30 rows, rep the 16 sts 5 times across row.

**Next row:** *K2, k2tog; rep from * to end (60 sts).

**Next row:** Work in k1, p1 twisted rib, dec 8 sts evenly across row (52 sts). Work next row in rib **.

### Shape thumb

**Row 1:** K24, pick up loop between last and next st and k into back of loop (m1k), k2, m1k, k26 (54 sts).

**Rows 2–4:** Stocking st.

**Row 5:** K24, m1k, k4, m1k, k26 (56 sts).

**Rows 6–8:** Stocking st.

**Row 9:** K24, m1k, k6, m1k, k26 (58 sts).

**Row 10:** P.

Work 8 more rows inc 2 sts as before in next and every foll alt row (66 sts).

Divide for thumb

**Row 1:** K40, cast on 1 st, turn.

**Row 2:** P17, cast on 1 st, turn.

Change to 2.75mm needles, then working on these 18 sts only, work 6 rows in moss st.

Cast off in moss st.

Join thumb seam.

With RS facing pick up and k2 sts from base of thumb and k to end (52 sts).

Cont in st st until glove measures 1¼in (3cm) from beg of thumb.

Change to 2.75mm needles and work 6 rows moss st, then cast off in moss st.

### Right-hand glove

Work as for left-hand glove to **.

### Shape thumb

**Row 1:** K26, m1k, k2, m1k, k24 (54 sts).

**Rows 2–4:** Stocking st.

**Row 5:** K26, m1k, k4, m1k, k24 (56 sts).

**Rows 6–8:** Stocking st.

**Row 9:** K26, m1k, k6, m1k, k24 (58 sts).

**Row 10:** P.

Work 8 rows inc 2 sts as before in next and every foll alt row (66 sts).

**Divide for thumb**

**Row 1:** K42, cast on 1 st, turn.

**Row 2:** P17, cast on 1 st, turn.

Complete to match thumb of left-hand glove.

With RS facing, pick up and k2 sts from base of thumb and k to end (52 sts).

Complete as for left-hand glove.

### Finishing

Tidy loose ends back into own colours. Join side seams of gloves. Steam seams. Using C, make 2 twisted cords 27in (68cm) long, thread through rib at wrist and tie in a bow.

# Bavarian flower chart
(16 sts x 20 rows)

*For hat: chart is read from right to left on all rows as hat is worked in the round.*

*For gloves: chart is read from right to left on RS rows and from left to right on WS rows.*

*1 square represents 1 stitch and 1 row.*

## Key to chart

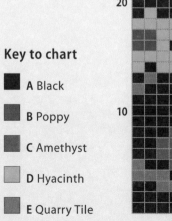

- **A** Black
- **B** Poppy
- **C** Amethyst
- **D** Hyacinth
- **E** Quarry Tile

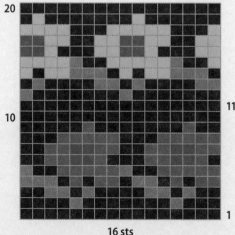

Commissioned in 1989 by Hugh
Ehrman of tapestry kit fame,
Acorn struck a patriotic cord with
the British public and paved the way
for a classic country look that has
since become my signature style.

# Acorn shawl-collared jacket

## Sizes
XS[S:M:L:XL]
**To fit bust**
34[36:38:40:42]in (86[91:96:101:106]cm)
**Actual measurements**
34[36:38:40:42]in (86[91:96:101:106]cm)
**Length**
25[25:25:26:26]in
(63.5[63.5:63.5:66:66]cm)
**Sleeve seam**
21[21:21½:22:22]in
(53.5[53.5:54.75:56:56]cm)
*Figures in square brackets refer to
larger sizes; where there is only one
set of figures this applies to all sizes.*

## You will need
Rowan Kid Classic
(153yds/140m per 50g ball)
3 balls 853 **Spruce (A)**
2[2:2:2:3] balls 872 **Earth (B)**
2 balls 852 **Victoria (C)**
7[7:8:8:8] balls 851 **Straw (D)**
1 ball 832 **Peat (E)**
1 ball 825 **Crushed Velvet (F)**
1 pair each of 3mm (US3:UK10)
and 3.75mm (US5:UK9) needles
1 x 3mm (US3:UK10) circular needle
7 x 19mm buttons
Stitch holders and markers

## Tension
23 sts and 26 rows to 4in (10cm)
over chart patt.
*Use larger or smaller needles if
necessary to obtain correct tension.*

## Pattern notes
This design uses the intarsia woven
method, see page 155.

## Back

Using 3mm needles and A cast on
110[114:120:126:132] sts.
Work 14 rows in k1, p1 twisted rib, rep
the foll stripe sequence four times,
carrying unused yarn up sides of work
and ending on C:

**Row 1:** B

**Row 2:** C

**Row 3:** A

Change to 3.75mm needles and refer
to chart and rep the 50 rows 3 times.
Centre chart as foll:
Work the last 2[4:7:10:13] sts of chart,
work the 53 sts twice, work the first
2[4:7:10:13] sts.
Cont in patt as set until work
measures 16¾[16¼:16¼:16¾:16¾]in
(42.5[41.25:41.25:42.5:42.5]cm) from
cast-on edge ending on a WS row.

### Shape armholes

Cast off 9[10:12:13:14] sts at beg of
next 2 rows (92[94:96:100:104] sts).
Cont in patt as set until work
measures 25[25:25:26:26]in
(63.5[63.5:63.5:66:66]cm) from cast-on
edge ending on WS row.
*NB: after three repeats of chart, cont
in D for few rows until correct length
is reached.*
Cast off.

## Pocket linings (make 2)

Using 3.75mm needles and D cast
on 28[28:30:30:30] sts. Work 4in
(10cm) in st st ending on WS row.
Place sts on a holder.

## Left front

Using 3mm needles and A cast on
55[57:60:63:66] sts and work 14 rows
in k1, p1 twisted rib in stripe sequence
as for back.
Change to 3.75mm needles and refer
to chart and work 24[24:26:26:26]
rows. Centre chart as foll:

**RS rows:** Work the last 2[4:7:10:13] sts

of chart, work the 53 sts.

**WS rows:** Work the 53 sts of chart,
work the first 2[4:7:10:13] sts.

### Place pocket lining

Patt 13[14:15:16:18] sts, slip next
28[28:30:30:30] sts onto a holder and
patt across 28[28:30:30:30] sts of first
pocket lining, patt rem 14[15:15:17:18] sts.
Cont in patt as set until work
measures 15[15:15:16:16]in
(38[38:38:40.75:40.75]cm) from cast-
on edge ending on RS row.

### Shape neck

Dec 1 st at beg of next and every
alt row 13[15:15:17:17] times, then
every foll 4th row 7[6:6:5:5] times
(26[26:27:28:30] sts).
At the same time, when work
measures 16¾[16¼:16¼:16¾:16¾]in
(42.5[41.25:41.25:42.5: 42.5]cm) from
cast-on edge ending on a WS row.

### Shape armhole

Cast off 9[10:12:13:14] sts, patt as set
to end.
Cont in patt as set until work
measures 25[25:25:26:26]in
(63.5[63.5:63.5:66:66]cm) from cast-on
edge ending on WS row (same as back
to end).
Change to 3mm needles and using
yarn A, k1 row, then work 12 rows in
k1, p1 twisted rib in stripe sequence
as for back.
Cast off in A.
Mark 6th row at armhole to indicate
natural shoulder line.

## Right front

Work as for left front reversing all
shapings and centring chart as foll:

**RS rows:** Work the 53 sts of chart, work
the first 2[4:7:10:13] sts.

**WS rows:** Work the last 2[4:7:10:13] sts
of chart, work the 53 sts of chart.

## Sleeves

Using 3mm needles and A cast on
54[54:54:60:60] sts. Work 18 rows k1,
p1 twisted rib in stripe sequence as
for back.
Change to 3.75mm needles and refer
to chart and rep the 50 rows twice,
then work the first 26 rows. Centre
chart as foll:
Work the last 1[1:1:4:4] sts, work the 53
sts of chart, work the first 0[0:0:3:3] sts.
At the same time, inc as foll:

**XS:** 1 st at both ends of 5th, then every
4th row 22 times, then every 6th row
twice (104 sts).

**S, M, L and XL:** 1 st at both ends of next
and foll 3 alt rows, then every foll 4th
row 24 times (110[110: 116:116] sts).
When 126 rows of chart are
completed, cont in D until work
measures 21½in (54.5cm).
Cast off.

## Finishing

### Collar and left front band

Using 3mm needles and A cast on
34 sts. Work 1 row k1, p1 twisted rib
in stripe sequence. Place marker at
the end of this row to indicate natural
shoulder line*.
Cont in stripe sequence, at the same
time casting on 8 sts at beg of next
and foll 9 alt rows (114 sts).
Next row: With RS of left front facing,
onto same needle pick up and k
98[98:98:104:104] sts from start of
front shaping to cast-on edge*. Work
a further 18 rows of stripe sequence
over all 212[212:212:218:218] sts.
Cast off loosely in rib in A.

## Right front band and collar

Using 3mm needles and A work 2 rows in k1, p1 twisted rib in stripe sequence, then place marker at end of row for shoulder line. Cont as for left side from * to *.

Work a further 11 rows over all 212[212:212:218:218] sts in stripe sequence.

**Buttonhole row:** Work 4 sts in patt as set, *cast off 4 sts, work 10[10:10:11:11] sts; rep from * twice, **cast off 4 sts, work 11[11:11:12:12] sts; rep from ** twice, ***cast off 4 sts, work 10[10:10:11:11] sts; rep from *** twice, cast off 4 sts, work 4 sts.

**Next row:** Work in patt as set, casting on these sts as you come to them. Work a further 4 rows in rib. Cast off loosely in rib in A.

## Pocket tops

Using 3mm needles, with RS facing and A, slip sts from holder onto needle. Work 1 row in st st then work 8 rows in k1, p1 twisted rib in stripe sequence. Cast off in rib in A. Tidy loose ends back into own colours. Press pieces lightly on WS avoiding ribbing. Sew pocket lining into position on WS and side edges of pocket top on to RS. Join shoulder seams. Sew cast off edge of sleeve into straight armhole edge, placing centre of sleeve at marker for natural shoulder line on row 6 of rib. Sew top 1½[1¾:2:2¼:2:½]in (4[4.5:5:5.75:6.5]cm) of sleeve to cast off edge at armhole forming a neat right angle. Join side seams and sleeve seams in one line. Join centre back seam of collar. Sew on buttons to correspond with buttonholes. Steam seams.

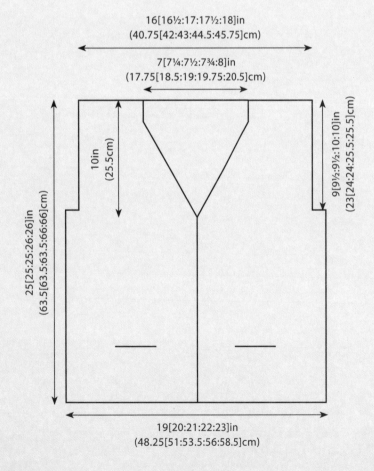

16[16½:17:17½:18]in
(40.75[42:43:44.5:45.75]cm)

7[7¼:7½:7¾:8]in
(17.75[18.5:19:19.75:20.5]cm)

10in
(25.5cm)

9[9½:9½:10:10]in
(23[24:24:25.5:25.5]cm)

25[25:25:26:26]in
(63.5[63.5:63.5:66:66]cm)

19[20:21:22:23]in
(48.25[51:53.5:56:58.5]cm)

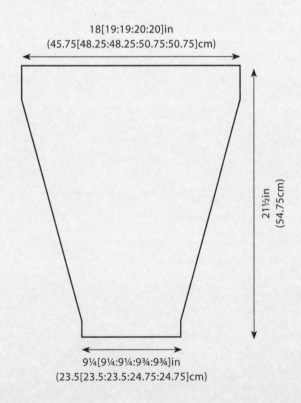

18[19:19:20:20]in
(45.75[48.25:48.25:50.75:50.75]cm)

21½in
(54.75cm)

9¼[9¼:9¼:9¾:9¾]in
(23.5[23.5:23.5:24.75:24.75]cm)

# Acorn chart (53 sts x 50 rows)

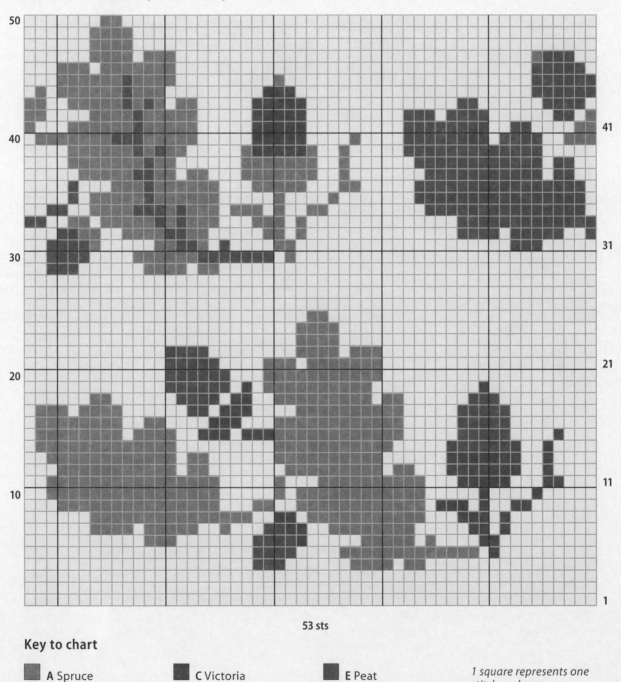

53 sts

## Key to chart

A Spruce  C Victoria  E Peat

B Earth  D Straw  F Crushed Velvet

*1 square represents one stitch and one row*

Vertical stripes are perfect for this garden favourite – echoing the vibrant linear quality of the plant. A popular *Woman's Weekly* design from 1988, this jacket is a useful statement piece in any wardrobe.

# Lavender jacket

## Sizes
XS[S:M:L:XL]
**To fit bust**
34[36:38:40:42]in (86[91:96:101:106]cm)
**Actual measurements**
36[38:40:42:44]in (91[96:101:106:111]cm)
**Length**
20[20:20:21:21]in (51[51:51:53.5:53.5]cm)
**Sleeve seam**
17[17:17½:18:18]in
(43[43:44.5:45.75:45.75]cm)
*Figures in brackets refer to larger sizes; where there is only one set of figures this applies to all sizes.*

## You will need
Rowan Pure Wool DK
(137yds/125m per 50g ball)
1[1:1:2:2] balls 030 **Damson (A)**
Rowan Revive
(137yds/125m per 50g ball)
2 balls 467 **Ironstone (B)**
Rowan Baby Alpaca DK
(109yds/100m per 50g ball)
1[1:1:2:2] balls 225 **Blossom (C)**
1 ball 222 **Menthol (D)**
1 ball 211 **Gooseberry (E)**
Rowan Felted Tweed
(191yds/175m per 50g ball)
3[3:3:4:4] balls 164 **Grey Mist (F)**
3 balls 151 **Bilberry (G)**
1 pair each of 3mm (US3:UK10) and
3.75mm (US5:UK9) needles
5 x ⅝in (17mm) buttons

## Tension
24 sts and 32 rows to 4in (10cm)
over chart patt.
*Use larger or small needles if necessary to obtain correct tension.*

## Pattern notes
This design uses the intarsia woven and linked methods, see page 155.

## Back

Using 3mm needles and A cast on 108[114:120:126:132] sts.

**Work 9 rows in garter st:** 1 row in A, 2 rows in B, 2 rows in C, 2 rows in B, 2 rows in A.

**Row 10 (WS):** P in A.

Change to 3.75mm needles and refer to chart and rep the 56 rows to end. Centre chart as foll:

**RS rows:** Work last 20[23:26:29:32] sts, work the 42 sts of chart twice, work first 4[7:10:13:16] sts.

**WS rows:** Work last 4[7:10:13:16] sts, work 42 sts of chart twice, work first 20[23:26:29:32] sts.

Cont in patt as set until work measures 11[10¾:10½:11¼:11]in (28[27.25:26.5:28.5:28]cm) from cast-on edge ending on a WS row.

**Shape armholes**

Cast off 5[5:5:6:6] sts at beg of next 2 rows. Then dec 1 st at both ends of next and every foll alt row 7[9:11:11:13] times (84[86:88:92:94] sts).

Cont in patt as set until work measures 19[19:19:20:20]in (48.25[48.25:48.25:51:51]cm ending on a WS row.

**Shape shoulders**

Cast off 8[9:9:9:9] sts at beg of next 2 rows.

Cast off 9[9:9:9:10] sts at beg of next 2 rows.

Cast off 9[9:10:10:10] sts at beg of next 2 rows.

Cast off rem 32[32:32:36:36] sts.

## Left front

Using 3mm needles and A cast on 57[57:60:63:66] sts and work 10 rows for welt in stripe sequence as for back. Change to 3.75mm needles and refer to chart and rep the 56 rows to end.

**Centre chart as foll:**

**RS rows:** Work last 37[37:32:28:26] sts, work the first 20[20:28:35:40] sts.

**WS rows:** Work last 20[22:28:34:40] sts, work first 37[35:32:29:26] sts.

*NB: for M and L sizes omit any flower sts on Bilberry panel at centre front.*

Cont in patt as set until work measures 11[10¾:10½:11¼:11]in (28[27.25:26.5:28.5:28]cm) from cast-on edge ending on a WS row.

**Shape armhole and neck**

Cast off 5[5:5:6:6] sts at beg of next row. Work 1 row. Then dec 1 st at beg of next and every foll alt row 10[9:11:11:13] times (42[43:44:46:47] sts).

At the same time, when work measures 11½[11½:11½:12:12]in (29.25[29.25:29.25:30.5:30.5]cm) from cast-on edge ending on RS row, shape neck:

Dec 1 st at beg of next, then every alt row 9[9:9:7:7] times, then every 4th row 6[6:6:10:10] times.

Cont in patt as set until work measures 19[19:19:20:20]in (48.25[48.25:48.25:51:51]cm ending on a WS row.

**Shape shoulder**

Cast off 8[9:9:9:9] sts at beg of next row. Work 1 row.

Cast off 9[9:9:9:10] sts at beg of next row. Work 1 row.

Cast off rem 9[9:10:10:10] sts.

## Right front

Work as for left front reversing all shapings and centring chart as foll:

**XS and S**

**RS rows:** Work last 35 sts, work the first 22 sts.

**WS rows:** Work the last 22 sts, work the first 35 sts.

**M, L and XL**

**RS rows:** Work last 1[8:13] sts, work the 42 sts of chart, work first 17[13:11] sts.

**WS rows:** Work the last 17[13:11] sts, work the 42 sts of chart, work first 1[8:13] sts.

## Sleeves

Using 3mm needles and A cast on 57[57:57:61:61] sts and work 10 rows for welt in stripe sequence as for back. Change to 3.75mm needles and refer to chart and rep the 56 rows to end. Centre chart as foll:

Work the last 36[36:36:38:38] sts, work the first 21[21:21:23:23] sts.

At the same time, inc 1 st at both ends of next, then every foll 6th row 0[0:0:0:2] times, then every foll 8th row 4[9:12:12:13] times, then every foll 10th row 8[4:2:2:0] times incorporating sts into patt in the 2 extra Grey Mist panels, but omitting flowers on the Bilberry panel at edges (83[85:87:91:93] sts).

Cont in patt as set until work measures 17[17:17½:17½:17½]in (43[43:44.5:44.5:44.5]cm) from cast-on edge ending on WS row.

**Shape sleeve cap**

Cast off 5[5:5:6:6] sts at beg of next 2 rows.

Then dec 1 st at both ends of every row 10[12:14:10:12] times, then every alt row 13[12:11:15:14] times, keeping patt correct as set. Work 1 row. Cast off 3 sts at beg of next 4 rows. Cast off rem 15[15:15:17:17] sts.

## Finishing

**Buttonhole band**

Using 3mm needles and A, with RS facing pick up and k 82[82:82:86:86] sts along front edge of right front to beginning of neck shaping. Knit 1 row. Change to B and knit 1 row.

**Buttonhole row:** K3, cast off 3 sts, (k15[15:15:16:16] sts, cast off 3 sts) 4 times, knit to end.

Change to C and knit to end, casting on 3 sts over cast off sts in previous row. Knit 1 row. Change to A and knit 1 row. Cast off in A.

**Buttonband**

Work to match buttonhole band omitting buttonholes.

**Collar**

Join shoulder seams. Using 3.25mm needles and A, with WS facing, beginning at centre of buttonband, pick up and k 56[56:56:59:59] sts along shaped edge of left front to shoulder, 32[32:32: 36:36] sts around back neck and k 56[56:56:59:59] sts down shaped edge of right front to centre of buttonhole band (144[144:144:154:154] sts). Knit 1 row.

Carrying yarn not in use up sides of collar work the following stripe sequence in garter stitch:
K 2 rows in B.
K 2 rows in C.
K 2 rows in B.
K 2 rows in A.
Rep last 8 rows 4 times more (40 rows).
Cast off.
Tidy loose ends back into own colours. Press pieces lightly on WS avoiding ribbing. Join side and sleeve seams in one line. Sew sleeve into armhole, placing any fullness evenly over sleeve cap. Sew on buttons opposite buttonholes. Steam seams.

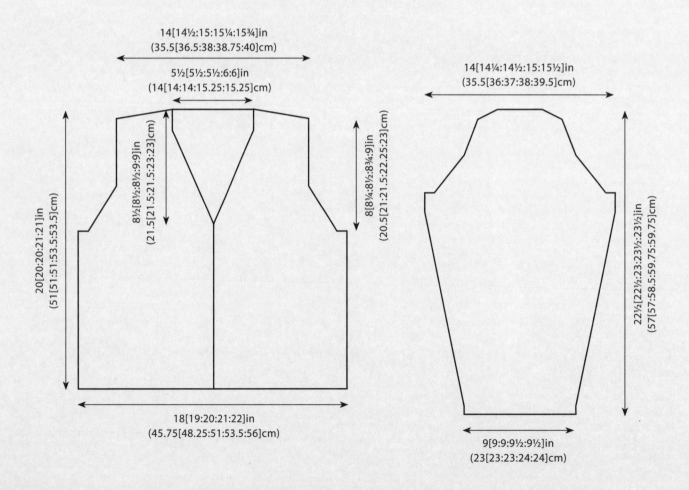

14[14½:15:15¼:15¾]in
(35.5[36.5:38:38.75:40]cm)

5½[5½:5½:6:6]in
(14[14:14:15.25:15.25]cm)

8½[8½:8½:9:9]in
(21.5[21.5:21.5:23:23]cm)

8[8¼:8½:8¾:9]in
(20.5[21:21.5:22.25:23]cm)

20[20:20:21:21]in
(51[51:51:53.5:53.5]cm)

18[19:20:21:22]in
(45.75[48.25:51:53.5:56]cm)

14[14¼:14½:15:15½]in
(35.5[36:37:38:39.5]cm)

22½[22½:23:23½:23½]in
(57[57:58.5:59.75:59.75]cm)

9[9:9:9½:9½]in
(23[23:23:24:24]cm)

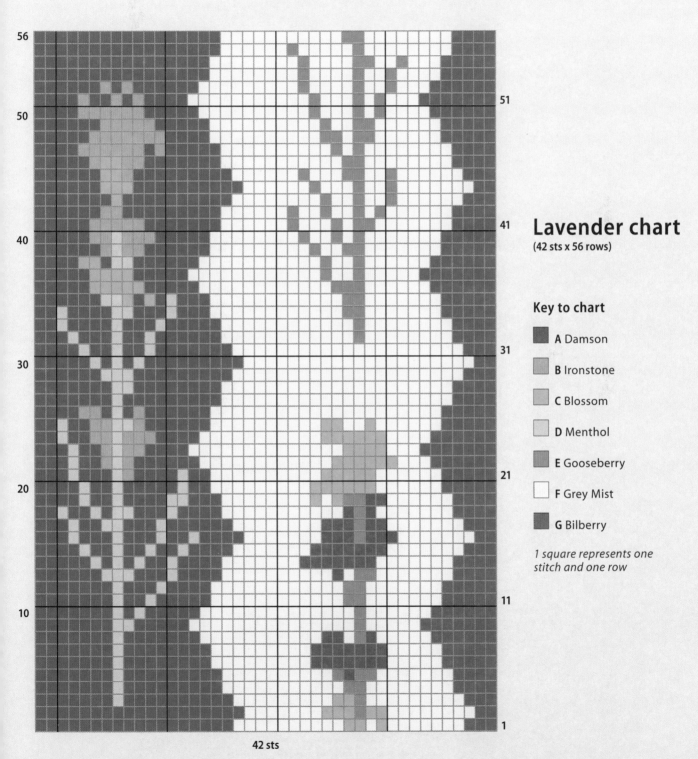

## Lavender chart
(42 sts x 56 rows)

### Key to chart

A Damson

B Ironstone

C Blossom

D Menthol

E Gooseberry

F Grey Mist

G Bilberry

*1 square represents one
stitch and one row*

42 sts

# The Welsh connection

**MOIRA VINCENTELLI,** PROFESSOR OF ART HISTORY AT ABERYSTWYTH UNIVERSITY IN WALES, DISCUSSES HOW KNITTING HAS BEEN AN INTEGRAL PART OF WELSH CULTURE FOR CENTURIES.

In the summer of 2010, the National Museum of Wales acquired the ultimate romantic evocation of Welsh knitting. Dating from 1860, William Dyce's painting shows two women knitting out on the mountains of Snowdonia; the standing figure is dressed in the iconic Welsh costume with red shawl and tall black hat. What kind of reality does it represent? Their passive demeanour chimes with a gender stereotype for knitting but the isolated and rugged setting for this domestic craft is more surprising.

Yet, in the nineteenth century knitting was to be seen outdoors. The eminent portability of the craft meant it could be done while minding animals or walking to market. Furthermore, while knitting is firmly established in the popular imagination as a female activity, men also knitted, especially where there was an economic benefit.

**Below left:** Welsh landscape with two women knitting, by William Dyce.

**Left:** Two women dressed in Welsh costume with a spinning wheel.

**Right:** Spinning and dyeing wool were skills that were passed down through families.

Wales was known for knitting as early as the sixteenth century, which is suggested by the name of a type of male beret. The Monmouth cap or Welsh wig, a precursor of the bobble hat, was gathered at the crown and sometimes had ear flaps. Knitting was widely practised in upland areas in Wales, where sheep's wool was readily available and could even be collected from bushes and fences. Women would spin and dye the wool and children learned to knit at an early age. By the eighteenth century the knitting of stockings had become a major industry, first developed by Welsh drovers who carried the knitted goods as an additional product to sell in England. However, later English hosiers visited the markets at Llanrwst, Bala or Tregaron specially to buy the stockings.

**Below:** Edward Llwyd of Bala, pictured circa 1875, was a local stocking knitter.

The eighteenth-century topographical writer and antiquary, Thomas Pennant recorded the market in Bala, in his *A Tour in Wales*, 1773, which was 'noted for its vast trade in woollen stockings and its great markets every Saturday morning when from two to five hundred pounds worth are sold every day.' He went on to describe another aspect of knitting. 'During winter the females, through love of society, often assemble at one another's house to knit, sit round a fire and listen to some old tale or some ancient song or the sound of a harp, and this is called cymmorth gweu or the knitting assembly.' Such sociable occasions have found a modern manifestation in the Stitch 'n' Bitch groups of the twenty-first century.

In spite of the apparent geographical connotations of 'raglan' sleeves and 'cardigan', both names are derived from aristocratic generals of the Crimean War (1854–6) and have no real connection with Wales. Nor has Wales given its name to any sweaters associated with the fishing industry, such as Aran or Guernsey, but a photograph from the National Museum of Wales records a Barmouth fisherman wearing a distinctive jumper with a heavy knitted yoke to give warmth to the upper body. The textile designer, Ann Sutton, reproduces this in her book *The Textiles of Wales* (Bellew, 1987) and designed an updated version with more specific Welsh references. By the late nineteenth century and the development of machine knitting, the hand-knitting industry in Wales was in decline. Hand knitting became the domain of the domestic knitter and of women.

For much of the twentieth century most women learned to knit whether at home or at school: for some it was torture, for others a joy. The ever-expanding market for women's magazines fed the interest in domestic prowess and romantic dreams and published knitting patterns for useful and decorative items from baby clothes to bathing costumes; tea-cosies to twinsets. From a certain feminist position, knitting, so strongly associated with women and the domestic arts, is also a symbol of female oppression – the classic activity of women in unpaid labour. But the new knitting of Sasha Kagan and fellow designers reclaimed the activity as something that was much more fun.

**Above:** Sasha was part of the early 1970s movement of people that sought a more rural, self-sufficient way of life.

In 1972 when Sasha Kagan settled in Wales, the move represented an idealistic choice for the time. The hedonism of the 'swinging sixties' began to give way to the more thoughtful ideologies of the 1970s and harder times leading up to the 'winter of discontent' in 1978–9. But in those years Wales offered the prospect of a better quality of life on a modest income. London salaries could quickly pay for interesting old properties, house prices were low and farmers preferred new bungalows to their old farmhouses. You could grow your own food, do up your house and buy beautiful pieces of pine to strip. You could have the best of the old alongside the modern amenities of running water, electricity and telephones.

Mid Wales has an important place in textile history. Llanidloes and Newtown had developed as centres for Welsh flannel production moving from cottage industry to industrial production by the first decade of the nineteenth century. The enterprising mill owner, Pryce Jones, established the first mail-order business at Newtown based on the new communication networks of the period: canals, railways and the postal service. After the 1960s the area became the headquarters of another major textile and design business: Laura Ashley. Echoing the values of the 'drop-out and back-to-nature movement' it promoted an alternative 'feminine' image. Aspects of this can also be seen in Sasha Kagan's inspiration taken from natural form and floral designs and the suggestions of new family values. Such designs are so different from the humble hand knits of 1950s childhoods. Her enterprise was a model for the times - eventually an international business working with many knitters from all around the country. Its reliance on the postal service and new communications makes an interesting link with Pryce Jones.

For Sasha Kagan the most exciting aspect of the work has always been the designing rather than the knitting itself but her knitting patterns, packs and workshops have brought pleasure to thousands of women (and some men). Knitting is a fulfilling activity in itself: the rhythmic handwork is therapeutic and soothing and feeds into the pleasure of seeing the patterns emerge and the delight in surprising colour combinations and varied textures. Knitting for babies, for children or for loved ones are further satisfactions and the bonding involved in learning

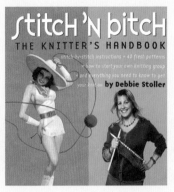

to knit is also important. According to one of the many blogs on the subject most people seem to be learning from their grandmothers these days. All this represents the traditional, feminine side of knitting.

However, knitting has another side to it – a much more subversive aspect. In contrast with her delicate floral imagery, some of Kagan's designs of the 1980s suggest a more edgy quality. Inspired by the postmodernism of the Italian design group, Memphis, Kagan developed her 'Flashes and Splashes' series – what she sometimes calls her 'angry' geometrics. Such work can link forward to the more political 'craft' work of Tracy Emin or Grayson Perry.

The subversion has also taken on the form of reclaiming the sociability of knitting. People come together in public places to reclaim knitting as a contemporary craft and a pleasurable group activity where the chat and mutual learning creates networks, cutting across age and gender. It harks back to the old cymmorth gweu (knitting assembly). For some this may be simple knitting in expensive yarns, for others the challenge of more advanced patterns. There are 'stitch 'n' bitch' groups across Wales but the movement goes one step further when it takes on the urban landscape. Guerilla knitting, also known as yarn bombing, started in the USA but Wales was quick to take up the challenge. On Valentine's Day, 2010, some Swansea citizens awoke to find their street decorated with knitted hearts and other woolly confections. Yarnarchy is a Swansea-based group who use knitting to leave their mark or tag. They vow never to make anything useful but aim to make people smile. An important extension to contemporary knitting, digital technology (such as Twitter and blogging) has become an essential element in the new knitting.

Wales has a proud history of knitting and Sasha Kagan has played an important part in it. Her career echoes aspects of the wider history of her times – from moving to a rural community in the 1970s to developing innovative marketing techniques and, above all, through her contribution as one of the leading designer knitters in the UK.

'A CALMER APPROACH REFLECTED THIS ERA
OF AUSTERITY – HAND KNITS USING TIMELESS IMAGERY
HELPED RE-INVENT THE CLASSIC INVESTMENT PIECE.'

1990 – 99

Influenced by my love of Art Nouveau and Pennsylvania Dutch folk art, this sinuous design is showcased by using vertical panels that open out into box pleats. First published by Rowan in *Sasha's Flower Book*.

# Tulip peplum jacket

## Sizes

XS[S:M:L:XL]

**To fit bust**

34[36:38:40:42]in (86[91:96:101:106]cm)

**Actual measurements**

34[36:38:40:42]in (86[91:96:101:106]cm)

**Length**

25½[25½:26½:26½:26½]in
(64.75[64.75:67:67:67]cm)

**Sleeve seam**

16½[16½:17:17:17]in (42[42:43:43:43]cm)

*Figures in square brackets refer to larger sizes; where there is only one set of figures this applies to all sizes.*

## You will need

Rowan Silky Tweed
(137yds/125m per 50g ball)
9[9:10:10:11] balls 754 **Tabby (A)**
Rowan Kid Classic
(153yds/140m per 50g ball)
1[1:1:1:1] ball 870 **Rosewood (B)**
1[1:1:1:1] ball 847 **Cherry Red (C)**
Rowan Pure Wool DK
(137yds/125m per 50g ball)
1[1:1:1:1] ball 30 **Damson (D)**
1[1:1:1:1] ball 26 **Hyacinth (E)**
Rowan Pure Silk DK
(137yds/125m per 50g ball)
1[1:1:2:2] ball 156 **Tranquil (F)**
1 pair extra long 3.25mm (US3:UK10)
and 1 pair 2.75mm (US2:UK12) needles
2.50mm (USC/2:UK12) crochet hook
11 x ⁹⁄₁₆in (15mm) buttons

## Tension

24 sts and 28 rows to 4in (10cm)
over chart patt.
*Use larger or smaller needles if necessary to obtain correct tension.*

## Pattern notes

This design uses the intarsia woven method, see page 155.

**Picot trim:**

*Ch3, sl st into same place, sl st across next 3 sts * rep from * to *. Fasten off.

**Box pleat (work over 40 sts)**

**Row 1(RS):** Sl purlwise, k38, sl 1 purlwise.

**Row 2:** P40.

Repeat rows 1 and 2 until 54 rows are completed.

## Back

Using 3.25mm needles and A cast on 246[252:258:264:270] sts.
Refer to chart and rep to end. Work the first 54 rows as foll:
Dec 1 st at both ends of 3rd and every foll 4th row 10[13:13:13:16] times, then every 6th row 5[3:4:4:2] times.
Set patt with pleats as foll:
**Row 1:** Working in st st and A, work 14[17:20:23:26] sts, work 25 sts of chart row 1, place marker, (using A make box pleat over next 40 sts, place marker, patt next 24 sts of chart row 1, place marker) twice, make box pleat over next 40 sts, place marker, patt rem 25 sts of chart row 1, using A work rem 14[17:20:23:26] sts in st st (246[252:258:264:270] sts).
**Row 55:** Cast off each of the 3 sets of 40 sts between markers as you come to them.
**Row 56:** Patt across all sts, taking care to pull yarn tightly as each patt block is brought together at pleat.
Cont until shaping is finished, then until work measures 12[12:12½:12½:12½]in (30.5[30.5: 31.75:31.75:31.75]cm) from cast-on edge ending on WS row (96[100:104:110:114] sts).
Then inc 1 st at both ends of next and every foll 12[8:6:6:5]th row 3[4:5:5:6] times (102[108:114:120:126] sts).
Cont in patt as set until work measures 17[17:17½:17½:17½]in (43[43:44.5:44.5:44.5]cm) from cast-on edge ending on WS row.

### Shape armholes

Cast off 6[6:6:9:9]sts at beg of next 2 rows (90[96:102:102:108] sts).
Cont in patt as set until work measures 25[25:26:26:26]in (63.5[63.5:66:66:66]cm) from cast-on edge ending on a WS row.

### Shape back neck

Work 40[43:46:46:49] sts in patt, turn.
Cast off 7[7:8:8:8] sts at beg of next row. Work 1 row.
Cast off 7[8:8:8:9] sts at beg of next row. Cast off rem 26[28:30:30:32] sts.
With RS facing, rejoin yarn to rem sts, cast off 10 sts and work to end. Work 1 row, then work to match first side rev shaping.

## Left front

Using 3.25mm needles and A cast on 103[106:109:112:115] sts.
Refer to chart and rep to end. Work the first 54 rows as foll:
Dec 1 st at beg of 3rd and every foll 4th row 10[13:13:13:16] times, then every 6th row 5[3:4:4:2] times.
Set patt with pleats as foll:
**Row 1:** Working in st st and A, work 14[17:20:23:26] sts, work sts 1–25 of chart row 1, place marker, using A make box pleat over next 40 sts, place marker, work sts 26–49 of chart row 1 (103[106:109:112:115] sts).
**Row 55:** Cast off the 40 sts between markers as you come to them.
**Row 56:** Patt across all sts, taking care to pull yarn tightly as each patt block is brought together at pleat.
Cont until shaping is finished, then on until work measures 12[12:12½:12½:12½]in (30.5[30.5: 31.75:31.75:31.75]cm) from cast-on edge ending on WS row (48[50:52:55:57] sts).
Then inc 1 st at beg of next and every foll 12[8:6:6:5]th row 3[4:5:5:6] times (51[54:57:60:63] sts).
Cont in patt as set until work measures 17[17:17½:17½:17½]in (43[43:44.5:44.5:44.5]cm) from cast-on edge ending on WS row.

### Shape armhole

Cast off 6[6:6:9:9] sts at beg of next 2 rows (45[48:51:51:54] sts).
Cont in patt as set until work measures 21½[21½:22½:22½:22½]in

(54.5[54.5:57:57:57]cm) from cast-on edge ending on a RS row.

### Shape front neck

Cast off 5 sts at beg of next row. Work 1 row.
Dec 1 st at beg of next and every row 10[12:14:14:16] times, then every alt row 4[3:2:2:1] times.
Cast off rem 26[28:30:30:32] sts.

## Right front

Work as for left front reversing all shapings and position pleat as foll:
**Row 1:** Work sts 50–73 of chart, place marker, using A make box pleat over next 40 sts, place marker, work sts 74–98 of chart, then working in st st and A, work 14[17:20:23:26] sts (103[106:109:112:115] sts).

## Sleeves

Using 3.25mm needles and A cast on 48[48:50:50:52] sts.
Refer to chart and rep the 86 rows to end, working as foll:
**Row 1(RS):** Using A and working in st st, work 12[12:13:13:14] sts, place marker, work sts 26–49 of chart, place marker, work a further 12[12:13:13:14] sts in st st in A.
Keeping patt correct as set, inc as foll:
**XS and S**
1 st at both ends of 3rd and every foll 4th row 27 times (102[102] sts).
**M, L and XL**
1 st at both ends of 3rd and every alt row 4[5, 3] times, then every foll 4th row 25[24:25] times (108[108:108] sts).
Cont in patt as set until sleeve measures 18[18:18½:18½:18½]in (45.75[45.75:47:47:47]cm) from cast-on edge and then cast off.

# Finishing

## Left front band

Using 2.75mm needles, with RS facing and A, pick up 4 sts for every 5 rows from neck shaping down to cast-on edge. Work 4 rows k1, p1 twisted rib, then cast off in rib.

## Right front band

Mark position of 7 buttonholes on right front: 1st just below start of neck shaping, last just above top of pleats and other five spaced evenly between. Work as for left front band making buttonholes in rows 2 and 3 by casting off 2 sts at markers and casting them on again on foll row.

## Neckband

Join shoulder seams.
Using 2.75mm needles RS facing and A, starting at right centre front, pick up and k 34[34:36:36:38] sts to shoulder seam, k 32[32:34:34:36] sts from back neck edge and k 34[34:36:36:38] sts down left side back to centre front (100[100:106:106:112] sts).

Work 4 rows k1, p1 twisted rib. Cast off in rib.

Tidy loose ends back into own colours. Sew down tops of box pleats. Press pieces lightly on WS. Sew cast off edge of sleeve seam into straight armhole edge. Sew top 1[1:1:1½:1½]in (2.5[2.5: 2.5:4:4]cm) of sleeve to cast-off edge of armhole forming a neat right angle. Join side seams and sleeve seams in one line leaving 1½in (3.5cm) open at cuff.

## Base trim

Using a 2.50mm crochet hook, WS facing and A join in yarn to bottom of right front band and work picot trim around hem. Fasten off.

## Cuff trim

Work as for base trim. Sew buttons opposite buttonholes. Sew a button to each side of cuff and make ½in (1cm) blanket stitch bar in between. Steam seams.

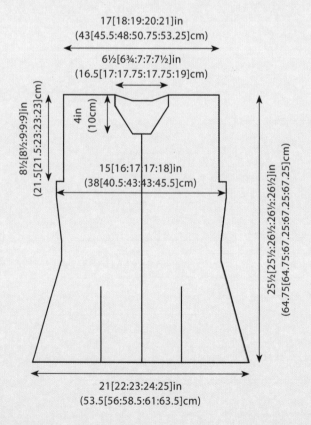

17[18:19:20:21]in
(43[45.5:48:50.75:53.25]cm)

6½[6¾:7:7:7½]in
(16.5[17:17.75:17.75:19]cm)

4in
(10cm)

8½[8½:9:9:9]in
(21.5[21.5:23:23:23]cm)

15[16:17:17:18]in
(38[40.5:43:43:45.5]cm)

25½[25½:26½:26½:26½]in
(64.75[64.75:67.25:67.25:67.25]cm)

21[22:23:24:25]in
(53.5[56:58.5:61:63.5]cm)

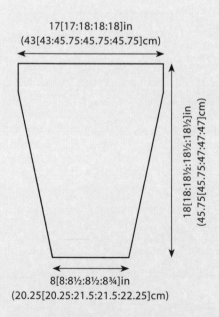

17[17:18:18:18]in
(43[43:45.75:45.75:45.75]cm)

18[18:18½:18½:18½]in
(45.75[45.75:47:47:47]cm)

8[8:8½:8½:8¾]in
(20.25[20.25:21.5:21.5:22.25]cm)

# Tulip chart (98 sts x 86 rows)

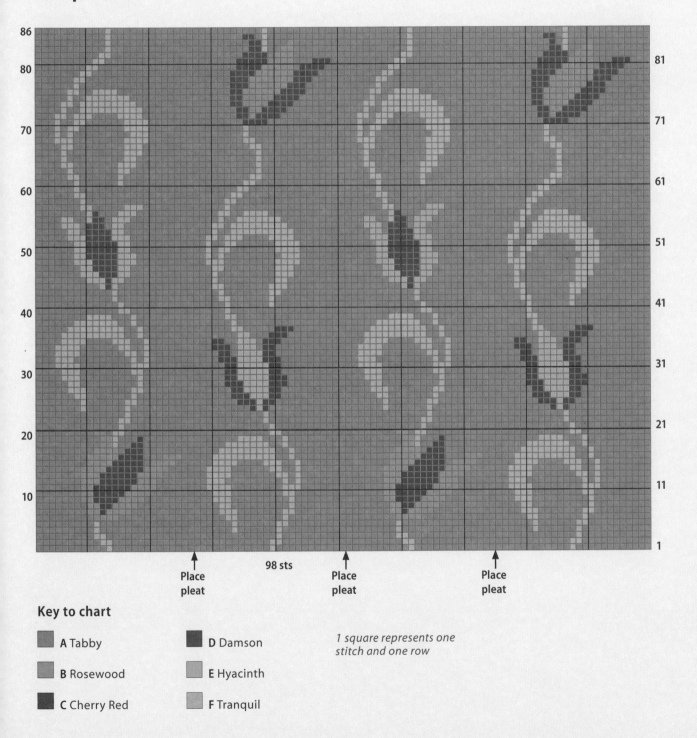

**Place pleat**

98 sts

**Place pleat**

**Place pleat**

## Key to chart

A Tabby

B Rosewood

C Cherry Red

D Damson

E Hyacinth

F Tranquil

*1 square represents one stitch and one row*

Pansy's popularity continues
on through many reincarnations
– a tunic in *Sasha's Flower Book*,
a sweater set in *Woman and Home*
magazine, a winter coat in *Country
Inspiration* and now a luxurious,
lacy pashmina.

# Pansy pashmina

## Size
**Length**
80in (203cm)
**Width**
16in (40cm)

## You will need
Rowan Organic Cotton 4-ply
(180yds/165m per 50g ball)
7 balls 751 **Natural (A)**
1 ball 761 **Cherry Plum (B)**
Rowan Siena 4-ply mercerized cotton
(153yds/140m per 50g ball)
1 ball 668 **Beacon (C)**
1 ball 666 **Chilli (D)**
1 ball 664 **Rosette (E)**
1 ball 670 **Sloe (F)**
1 ball 658 **Floret (G)**
1 ball 662 **Flounce (H)**
1 ball 659 **Oak (I)**
Rowan Wool Cotton
(123yds/113m per 50g ball)
1 ball 974 **Freesia (J)**
1 pair each of 2.75mm (US2:UK12) and
3mm (US3:UK10) needles

## Tension
28 sts and 36 rows to 4in (10cm)
over chart patt using 3mm needle.
*Use larger or smaller needles if
necessary to obtain correct tension.*

## Pattern notes
This design uses the intarsia woven
method, see page 155.

## Pashmina

### Top zigzag edging

*Using 2.75mm needles and A cast on
2 sts using the thumb method.
**Row 1 (RS):** K2.
**Row 2:** Yo, k2.
**Row 3:** Yo, k3.
**Row 4:** Yo, k4.
**Row 5:** Yo, k5.
**Row 6:** Yo, k6.
**Row 7:** Yo, k7.
**Row 8:** Yo, k8.
**Row 9:** Yo, k9 (10 sts).
Cut yarn and leave point on needle.
On the same needle cast on 2 sts and
work second point as first.

Work 11 points altogether.
On last point do not break yarn but
turn and k across all points on needle.
Work 6 rows garter stitch inc 1 st on
last row (111 sts)*.
Change to 3mm needles and refer
to chart, working chart as foll:
Work 5 sts in garter st, work the 101
sts of chart, work 5 sts in garter st.
Repeat the 64 rows of chart 11 times,
keeping 5 sts of garter st correct at
each side, then work rows 1 and 2
to finish.
Leave stitches on a spare needle.

## Finishing

### Bottom zigzag edging

Work as for top zigzag edging from *
to *.
With right sides facing, hold edging
in front of pashmina and cast off 2 sts
tog across row (three-needle cast-off).
Tidy loose ends back into own colours.
Press piece lightly on WS avoiding
borders. Using A make 22 5in (13cm)
long tassels and attach to points of
zigzag edging.

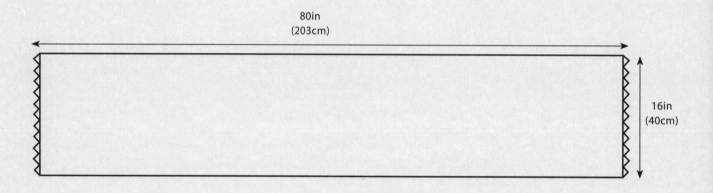

80in
(203cm)

16in
(40cm)

# Pansy chart (101 sts x 64 rows)

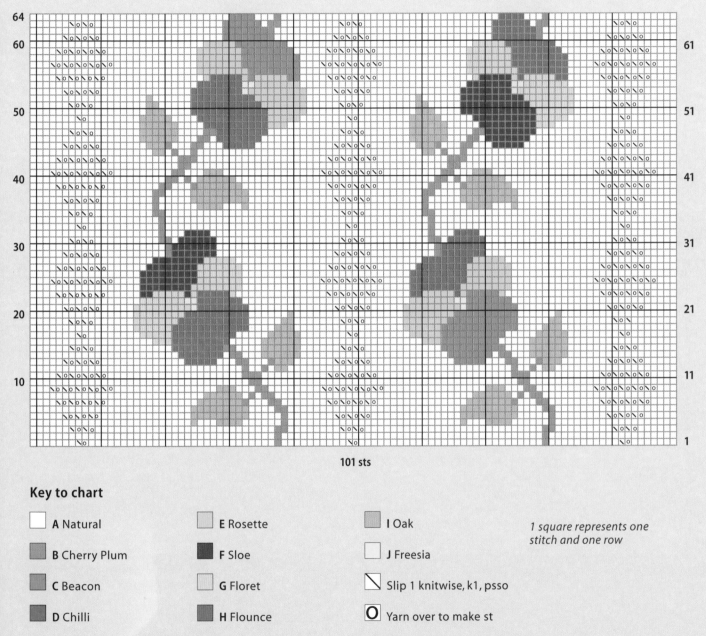

101 sts

## Key to chart

| | | |
|---|---|---|
| **A** Natural | **E** Rosette | **I** Oak |
| **B** Cherry Plum | **F** Sloe | **J** Freesia |
| **C** Beacon | **G** Floret | ⟍ Slip 1 knitwise, k1, psso |
| **D** Chilli | **H** Flounce | **O** Yarn over to make st |

*1 square represents one stitch and one row*

Wildflower was commissioned by Stephen Sheard, founder of Rowan yarns, to commemorate the company's 10th anniversary. It is one of my favourite designs, with tiny delicate blooms inspired by Liberty print.

# Wildflower cropped cardigan

## Sizes
XS[S:M:L:XL]
**To fit bust**
34[36:38:40:42]in
(86[91:96:101:106]cm)
**Actual measurements**
36[38:40:42:44]in
(91.5[96.5:101.5:106.5:111.75]cm)
**Length**
18[18:18:19:19]in
(45.75[45.75:45.75:48.25:48.25]cm)
**Sleeve seam**
17¼in (44cm)
*Figures in square brackets refer to larger sizes; where there is only one set of figures this applies to all sizes.*

## You will need
Rowan Siena 4-ply cotton
(153yds/140m per 50g ball)
7[7:7:8:8] balls 659 **Oak (A)**
2 balls 652 **Cream (B)**
1 ball 668 **Beacon (C)**
1[1:2:2:2] balls 661 **Greengage (D)**
1 ball 658 **Floret (E)**
Rowan Wool Cotton
(123yds/113m per 50g ball)
1 ball 974 **Freesia (F)**
1 pair each of 2.75mm (US2:UK12) and
3.25mm (US3:11) needles
6 buttons

## Tension
28 sts and 34 rows to 4in (10cm)
over chart patt.
*Use larger or smaller needles if necessary to obtain correct tension.*

## Pattern notes
This design uses the intarsia woven method, see page 155.
**Beaded rib**
Multiple of 5 + 2
**Row 1:** *P2, k1, p1, k1; rep from * to last 2 sts, p2.
**Row 2:** *k2, p3; rep from * to last 2 sts, k2.

## Back

Using 2.75mm needles and A cast on 122[127:137:147:152] sts and work 3in (7.5cm) in beaded rib, inc 4[5:3:1:2] sts evenly on final row (126[132:140:148:154] sts).

Change to 3.25mm needles and refer to chart, working all 52 rows once, then rep rows 16–52 to end. Centre chart as foll:

Work the last 3[6:10:14:17] sts, work the 40 sts of chart 3 times, work the first 3[6:10:14:17] sts.

Cont in patt as set until work measures 10½[10½:10½:11:11]in (26.75[26.75:26.75:28:28]cm) from cast-on edge ending on a WS row.

### Shape armholes

Cast off 3 sts at beg of next 2 rows and 2[2:2:3:3] sts at beg of foll 2 rows (116[122:130:136:142] sts).

Cont in patt as set until work measures 18[18:18:19:19]in (45.75[45.75:45.75:48.25:48.25]cm) from cast-on edge ending on a WS row.

### Shape shoulders

Cast off 40[43:47:49:52] sts at beg of next 2 rows. Cast off rem 36[36:36:38:38] sts.

## Left front

Using 2.75mm needles and A cast on 62[62:67:72:77] sts. Work 3in (7.5cm) in beaded rib as for back, inc 1[4:3:2:0] sts evenly on last row (63[66:70:74:77] sts).

Change to 3.25mm needles and refer to chart, working all 53 rows once, then rep rows 16–52 to end. Centre chart as foll:

**RS rows:** Work the last 3[6:10:14:17] sts, work the 40 sts of chart once, work the first 20 sts.

**WS rows:** Work the last 20 sts, work the 40 sts of chart once, work the first 3[6:10:14:17] sts.

Cont in patt as set until work measures 8½[8½:8½:9½:9½]in (21.5[21.5:21.5:24:24]cm) from cast-on edge ending on RS row.

### Shape neck

Dec 1 st at beg of next and every 4th row 18[18:18:19:19] times in all. At the same time work armholes when work measures 10½[10½:10½:11:11]in (26.75[26.75:26.75:28:28]cm) from cast-on edge ending on a WS row.

### Shape armholes

Cast off 3 sts at beg of next row. Work 1 row. Cast off 2[2:2:3:3] sts at beg of foll row (57[61:65:68:71] sts).

Cont in patt as set until work measures 18[18:18:19:19]in (45.75[45.75:45.75:48.25:48.25]cm from cast-on edge ending on a WS row. Cast off rem 40[43:47:49:52] sts.

## Right front

Work as for left front reversing all shapings. Centre chart as foll:

**RS rows:** Work the last 20 sts, work the 40 sts of chart once, work the first 3[6:10:14:17] sts.

**WS rows:** Work the last 3[6:10:14:17] sts, work the 40 sts of chart once, work the first 20 sts.

## Sleeves

Using 2.75mm needles and A cast on 52[52:52:57:57] sts and work 3in (7.5cm) in beaded rib as for back, inc 8[8:8:9:9] sts evenly across last row (60[60:60:66:66] sts).

Change to 3.25mm needles and refer to chart, working all 53 rows once, then rep rows 16–52 to end. Centre chart as foll:

Work the last 10[10:10:13:13] sts, work the 40 sts of chart once, work the first 10[10:10:13:13] sts.

At the same time inc 1 st at both ends of first chart row, then every foll 6th row 9[9:9:7:7]times, then every foll 4th row 14[14:14:17:17] times, taking extra sts into patt as they occur (108[108:108:116:116] sts).

Cont until work measures 18½in (47cm) from cast-on edge ending on WS row. Cast off.

## Finishing

Join shoulder seams.

### Buttonhole band

Using 2.75mm needles, with RS facing and A pick up and k58[58:58:67:67] sts from base of welt up right front edge to start of shaping, 66 sts up right front slope and 18[18:18:19:19] sts from half back neck (142[142:142:152:152] sts). Mark position of 6 buttonholes: the first 4 sts up from base of welt, next one at top of welt, one spaced evenly between these (3 buttonholes on welt), the next at start of neckline shaping and the final 2 spaced evenly between that and top of welt.

Work 6 rows beaded rib making 6 buttonholes on rows 3 and 4 at markers by casting off 2 sts for each hole and casting on these sts again on foll row.

## Button band

Work as for buttonhole band omitting buttonholes.

Tidy loose ends back into own colours. Press pieces lightly on WS avoiding ribbing. Sew cast off edge of sleeve into straight armhole edge. Sew top ¾in (2cm) of sleeve to cast-on edge of armhole. Join side seams and sleeve seams in one line. Steam seams. Sew on buttons opposite buttonholes.

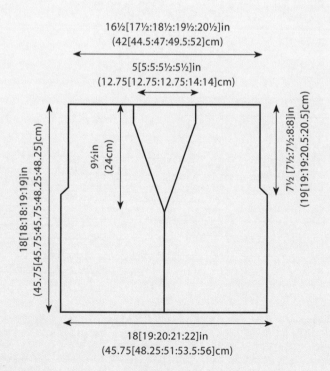

16½[17½:18½:19½:20½]in
(42[44.5:47:49.5:52]cm)

5[5:5:5½:5½]in
(12.75[12.75:12.75:14:14]cm)

9½in
(24cm)

18[18:18:19:19]in
(45.75[45.75:45.75:48.25:48.25]cm)

7½ [7½:7½:8:8]in
(19[19:19:20.5:20.5]cm)

18[19:20:21:22]in
(45.75[48.25:51:53.5:56]cm)

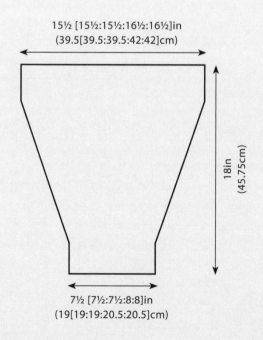

15½ [15½:15½:16½:16½]in
(39.5[39.5:39.5:42:42]cm)

18in
(45.75cm)

7½ [7½:7½:8:8]in
(19[19:19:20.5:20.5]cm)

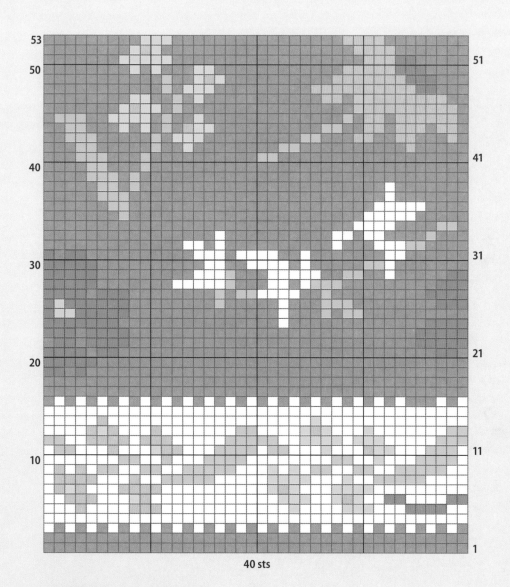

40 sts

# Wildflower chart

(40 sts x 53 rows)

## Key to chart

| | **A** Oak | | **C** Beacon | | **E** Floret |
|---|---|---|---|---|---|
| | **B** Cream | | **D** Greengage | | **F** Freesia |

*1 square represents one stitch and one row*

Clusters of hazelnuts adorn this V-neck jacket design, making a perfect outer layer for early autumn afternoons. The luxurious UK Alpaca yarn in gorgeous natural colours is spun in Devon, England.

# Hazelnut V-neck jacket

## Sizes
XS[S:M:L:XL]
**To fit bust**
34[36:38:40:42]in (86[91:96:101:106]cm)
**Actual measurements**
36[38:40:42:44]in (91[96:101:106:111]cm)
**Length**
29[29:29½:29½:30]in
(74[74:75:75:76.25]cm)
**Sleeve seam**
17½[17½:18:18:18½]in
(44.5[44.5:45.75:45.75:47]cm)
*Figures in square brackets refer to larger sizes; where there is only one set of figures this applies to all sizes.*

## You will need
UK Alpaca DK
(144yds/132m per 50g ball):
3[3:4:4:4] balls 12 **Fawn (A)**
8[8:9:9:9] balls 11 **Champagne (B)**
3[3:3:3:3] balls 13 **Chocolate (C)**
1[1:1:1:1] ball 14 **Silver Grey (D)**
1 pair each of 3.25mm (US3:UK10) and 4mm (US6:UK8) needles
3.25mm (US3:UK10) and 3mm (US2:UK11) long circular needles
Stitch holder, markers
3 x 1¼in (3cm) buttons

## Tension
25 sts and 30 rows to 4in (10cm) over chart patt using 4mm needles. *Use larger or smaller needles if necessary to obtain correct tension.*

## Pattern notes
This design uses the intarsia woven method, see page 155.

## Back

Using 3.25mm needles and A cast on 112[120:128:132:140] sts.
Work 10 rows 2-colour moss st as foll:
**Row 1:** *K2 with C, p2 with A; rep from * to end.
**Row 2:** *P2 with C, k2 with A; rep from * to end.
Rep these 2 rows.
Change to 4mm needles and refer to chart, centring it as foll:
Work last 16[0:4:6:10], work 40 sts 2[3:3:3:3] times, work first 16[0:4:6:10] sts.
At the same time dec 1 st at both ends of 21[21:19:19:21]st row, then ev foll 16th row 5 times, keeping chart correct (100[108:116:120:128] sts).
Cont as set, keeping patt correct until work measures 16¾[16¾:16¼:16¼:16¾]in (42.5[42.5: 41.25:41.25:42.5]cm) from cast-on edge ending with WS row, then inc as foll:
Inc 1 st at both ends of next, then every foll alt row 1[0:0:0:0] times, then every foll 4th row 4[4:1:4:2] times, then every 6th row 0[0:3:1:2] times (112[118:126:132:138]sts).
Cont in patt as set until work measures 20¼[20:20¼:20¼:20½]in (51.5[51:51.5:51.5: 52]cm) from cast-on edge ending on WS row.
### Shape armholes
Cast off 6[7:7:8:8] sts at beg of next 2 rows.
Dec 1 st at both ends of next and every alt row 9[10:12:13:14] times in all (82[84:88:90:94] sts).
Cont as set until work measures 28½[28½:29:29:29½]in (72.5[72.5:73.75:73.75:75]cm) from cast-on edge ending with WS row.
### Shape shoulders
Cast off 12[13:13:14:14] sts at beg of next 2 rows.
Cast off 13[13:14:14:15] sts at beg of next 2 rows.

Place rem 32[32:34:34:36] sts on holder.

## Left front

Using 3.25mm needles and A, cast on 56[60:64:66:70] sts.
Work 10 rows 2-colour moss st as before for XS, S, M, for L and XL work as foll:
**Row 1:** *K2 with C, p2 with A; rep from * to last 2 sts, k2 with C.
**Row 2:** K2 with A, *P2 with C, k2 with A; rep from * to end.
Change to 4mm needles and refer to chart, centring it as foll:
Work last 16[0:4:6:10], work 40 sts, work first 0[20:20:20:20] sts.
At the same time dec 1 st at beg of 21[21:19:19:21]st row, then every foll 16th row 5 times, keeping chart correct (50[54:58:60:64] sts).
Cont as set, keeping patt correct until work measures 16¾[16¾:16¼:16¼:16¾]in (42.5[42.5: 41.25:41.25:42.5]cm) from cast-on edge ending with WS row, then inc as foll:
Inc 1 st at beg of next, then every foll alt row 1[0:0:0:0] times, then every foll 4th row 4[4:1:4:2] times, then every 6th row 0[0:3:1:2] times (56[59:63:66:69]sts).
At the same time cont until work measures 19[19:19½:19½:20]in (48.25[48.25:49.5:49.5:51]cm) from cast-on edge ending on RS row.
### Shape neck
#### XS, S, M and L
Dec 1 st at beg of next and every foll 4th row 16[16:17:17] times (25[26:27:28] sts).
#### XL
Dec 1 st at beg of next, then every foll alt row twice, then every 4th row 15 times (29 sts).
At the same time cont until work measures 20¼[20:20¼:20¼:20½]in

(51.5[51:51.5:51.5: 52]cm) from cast-on edge ending on WS row.
### Shape armhole
Cast off 6[7:7:8:8] sts at beg of next row. Work 1 row.
Dec 1 st at beg of next and every alt row 9[10:12:13:14] times in all (41[42:44:45:47] sts).
Cont as set until work measures 28½[28½:29:29:29½]in (72.5[72.5:73.75:73.75:75]cm) from cast-on edge ending with WS row.
### Shape shoulders
Cast off 12[13:13:14:14] sts at beg of next row. Work 1 row.
Cast off 13[13:14:14:15] sts at beg of next row.

## Right front

Work as for left front reversing shapings and centring chart as foll:
Work last 0[20:20:20:20], work 40 sts, work first 16[0:4:6:10] sts.

## Sleeves

Using 3.25mm needles and A cast on 64[64:64:68:68] sts.
Work 3in (7.75cm) in 2-colour moss st as for back.
Change to 4mm needles and refer to chart, centring it as foll:
Work the last 12[12:12:14:14] sts of chart, work the 40, work the first 12[12:12:14:14] sts.
At the same time inc 1 st at both ends of next, then every foll 6th row 0[6:4:0:0] times, then every foll 8th row 12[8:10:13:13] times (90[94:94:96:96] sts).
Cont until work measures 17½[17½:18:18½:18½]in (44.5[44.5:45.75:47:47]cm) from cast-on edge ending on WS row.

### Shape sleeve cap

Cast off 6[7:7:8:8] sts at beg of next 2 rows.

Dec 1 st at both ends of every row 14[16:14:14:14] times, then every alt row 12[11:12:12:12] times. Cast off 3 sts at beg of next 4 rows.

Cast off rem 14[14:16:16:16] sts.

## Finishing

Join shoulder seams.

### Front band

With RS facing, using 3.25mm circular needle and A, beg at cast-on edge of right front and end at cast-on edge of left front, pick up and k 196[196:197:197:200] sts up centre right front to shoulder, k across 32[32:34:34:36] sts on holder at back neck, and pick up and k 196[196:197:197:200] sts down left front (424[424:428:428:436] sts).

Work 4 rows bi-colour moss st as for back starting with row 2.

Mark position of 3 buttonholes on right front band, the first just after the V point, the foll 2 with 16 sts between (4 sts will make the hole, then 12 sts between).

**Next row:** Work as set, casting off 4 sts at markers for each buttonhole.

**Next row:** Cast on these sts as you come to them.

Work 3 more rows rib.

### Front band facing

Change to 3mm circular needle.

**Next row:** K using A.

**Next row:** K using A (to form fold line).

Work in st st for 10 rows making buttonholes to correspond with those on front band. Cast off on 3.25mm circular needle.

Tidy loose ends back into own colours. Press pieces lightly on WS.

Insert sleeves placing any fullness evenly over sleeve cap. Join sleeve and side seams in one line. Turn front band facings at fold line to inside and hem in place. Oversew buttonholes and sew buttons on left front band opposite buttonholes. Steam seams.

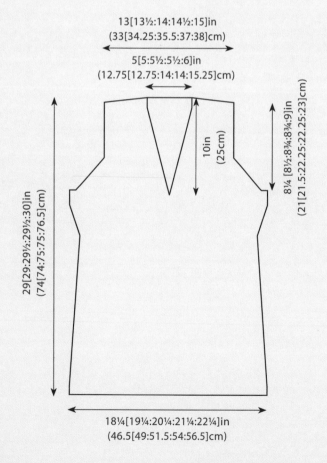

13[13½:14:14½:15]in
(33[34.25:35.5:37:38]cm)

5[5:5½:5½:6]in
(12.75[12.75:14:14:15.25]cm)

10in
(25cm)

8¼ [8½:8¾:8¾:9]in
(21[21.5:22.25:22.25:23]cm)

29[29:29½:29½:30]in
(74[74:75:75:76.5]cm)

18¼[19¼:20¼:21¼:22¼]in
(46.5[49:51.5:54:56.5]cm)

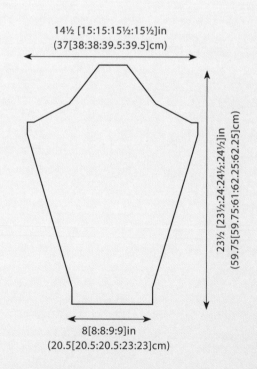

14½ [15:15:15½:15½]in
(37[38:38:39.5:39.5]cm)

23½ [23½:24:24½:24½]in
(59.75[59.75:61:62.25:62.25]cm)

8[8:8:9:9]in
(20.5[20.5:20.5:23:23]cm)

# Hazelnut chart (40 sts x 44 rows)

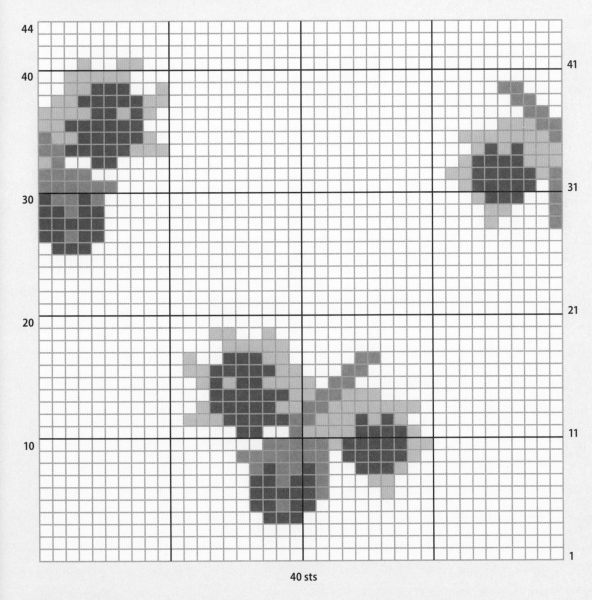

40 sts

## Key to chart

 **A** Fawn

**B** Champagne

**C** Chocolate

**D** Silver Grey

*1 square represents one stitch and one row*

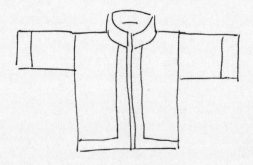

Ethnic shapes add a timeless dimension and the proportions of this kimono make a perfect canvas for a large graphic print. This design was first seen in *Woman and Home* magazine in 1989.

# Oriental flowers kimono

## Sizes
S[M:L]
**To fit bust**
34–40[42–48:50–56]in
(86.5–101.5[106.5–122:127–142.25]cm)
**Actual measurements**
46[54:62]in (117[137:157.5]cm)
**Length**
28½[29:29½]in (72.5[73.75:75]cm)
**Sleeve seam**
17in (43cm)
*Figures in square brackets refer to larger sizes; where there is only one set of figures this applies to all sizes.*

## You will need
Rowan Baby Alpaca
(109 yds/100m per 50g ball)
3 balls 225 **Blossom (A)**
1 ball 215 **Spring Leaf (B)**
Rowan Felted Tweed
(191yds/175m per 50g ball)
6[7:8] balls 152 **Watery (C)**
3 balls 164 **Grey Mist (D)**
Rowan Pure Silk DK
(137yds/125m per 50g ball)
1[2:2] balls 151 **Bone (E)**
Rowan Kid Classic
(153yds/140m per 50g ball)
1[2:2] balls 854 **Tea Rose (F)**
Rowan Wool Cotton
(123yds/113m per 50g ball)
2 balls 951 **Tender (G)**
2 balls 974 **Freesia (H)**

1 pair each of 2.75mm (US2:UK12) and 3.75mm (US5:UK9) needles
Stitch holder and markers

## Tension
26 sts and 28 rows to 4in (10cm) over chart pattern.
*Use larger or smaller needles if necessary to obtain correct tension.*

## Pattern notes
This design uses the intarsia woven method, see page 155.

## Back

Using 2.75mm needles and A cast on 150[176:200] sts and work 3¾in (9.5cm) in st st ending on a WS row.

**Next row:** K1 * yf, k2tog; rep from * to last st, k1.

**Next row:** Purl.

Change to 3.75mm needles and refer to chart and work the first 30 rows, centring chart as foll:

**RS rows:** Work 100 sts of chart 1[1:2] times, work the first 50[76:0] sts.

**WS rows:** Work the last 50[76:0] sts, work 100 sts of chart 1[1:2] times.

Cont with chart, rep rows 31–88 three times (174 rows).

Centre chart for these rows as foll:

**RS rows:** Work 0[13:25] sts in st st in C, work the 100 sts of chart, work the first 50 sts, work 0[13:25] sts in st st in C.

**WS rows:** Work 0[13:25] sts in st st in C, work the last 50 sts of chart, work the 100 sts of chart, work 0[13:25] sts in st st in C.

Cont in patt as set until work measures 28½[29:29½]in (72.5[73.75:75]cm) from picot line ending on WS row, working any extra rows after patt row 174 in st st in C.

**Shape shoulders**

Using C cast off 50[63:75] sts at beg of next 2 rows.

Leave rem 50 sts on holder.

## Left front

Using 2.75mm needles and A cast on 50[64:76] sts and work 3¾in (9.5cm) in st st ending with WS row.

**Next row:** K1 *yf, k2tog; rep from * to last st, k1.

**Next row:** Purl, dec 1 st at beg of row on M and L sizes (50[63:75] sts).

Change to 3.75mm needles and refer to chart and work the first 30 rows, centring chart as foll:

## S and L

**RS rows:** Work first 50[75] sts of chart.

**WS rows:** Work the last 50[75] sts.

**M**

**RS rows:** Work last 24 sts of chart, work the first 39 sts.

**WS rows:** Work the last 39 sts, work the first 24 sts.

Cont with chart, rep rows 31–88 three times (174 rows).

Centre chart for these rows as foll:

**RS rows:** Work 0[7:13] sts in st st in C, work first 50 sts of chart, work 0[7:13] sts in st st in C.

**WS rows:** Work 0[7:13] sts in st st in C, work last 50 sts of chart, work 0[7:13] sts in st st in C.

*NB: work any extra rows at shoulder in st st in C.*

Cont in patt as set until work measures 28½[29:29½]in (72.5[73.75:75]cm) from picot line ending on WS row, working any extra rows after patt row 174 in st st in C. Cast off.

## Right front

Work as for left front centring chart for first 30 rows as foll:

## S and L

**RS rows:** Work last 50[75] sts of chart.

**WS rows:** Work the first 50(75] sts.

**M**

**RS rows:** Work last 39 sts of chart, work the first 24 sts.

**WS rows:** Work the last 24 sts, work the first 39 sts.

Centre the chart for rows 31–88 as foll:

**RS rows:** Work 0[7:13] sts in st st in C, work last 50 sts of chart, work 0[7:13] sts in st st in C.

**WS rows:** Work 0[7:13] sts in st st in C, work first 50 sts of chart, work 0[7:13] sts in st st in C.

## Sleeves

Using 2.75 mm needles and A cast on 100[104:110] sts and work 4 rows in st st.

**Next row:** K1 *yf, k2tog; rep from * to last st, k1.

**Next row:** Purl.

Change to 3.75mm needles and refer to chart and work first 30 rows, centring chart as foll:

Work the last 0[2:5] sts, work the 100 sts, work the first 0[2:5] sts.

Cont with chart to row 88, then rep rows 31–60 (118 rows).

Centre chart for these rows as foll:

Work 0[2:5] sts in st st in C, work the 100 sts of chart, work 0[2:5] sts in st st in C. Cast off.

## Finishing

### Left front band

Place marker 3in (7.5cm) down from shoulder to mark neck edge.

Using 3.75mm needles and A, with RS facing, starting at start of neck shaping and ending at picot row, pick up and k160[164:168] sts down left front edge.

**Next row:** Purl.

Turn chart upside down and begin at row 29, working backwards to row 1, centring chart as foll:

**Rows 29, 28, 2 & 1:** Work last 30[32:34] sts of chart, work the 100 sts, work first 30[32:34] sts.

**Rows 27–3:** Work 5[7:9] sts in st st in D, work 100 sts of chart, then work first 50 sts, work 5[7:9] sts in st st in D.

At the same time shape band on rows 29–20:

Dec 1 st at neck edge on next and every row 10 times, keeping patt correct as set.

Cont without shaping through rows 19–1.

**Next row:** Purl in A.

**Next row:** K1 *yf, k2tog; rep from * to last st, k1.
Change to 2.75mm needles and cont in A. Beg with a WS (p) row, work 29 rows in st st, inc 1 st at neck edge on rows 20–29. Cast off.

### Right front band

Work as for left front band picking up sts starting at picot row up right front edge ending at marker. Reverse all shapings.

### Collar

Join shoulder seams.
Using 3.75mm needles, with RS facing and A, beg at picot row on right front band, pick up and k50 sts up right front neck edge to shoulder seam, k across 50 sts on holder at back neck, pick up and k50 sts down left neck edge to picot row on left front band (150 sts).
**Next row:** Purl.
Refer to chart and work rows 29–1, centring chart as foll:
**RS rows:** Work the 100 sts of chart, work the first 50 sts.
**WS rows:** Work the last 50 sts, work the 100 sts of chart.
**Next row:** Purl.
**Next row:** K1 *yf, k2tog; rep from * to last st, k1.
Change to 2.75mm needles and cont with A, work 3¾in (9.5cm) in st st. Cast off.

### Collar edgings

Using 2.75mm needles, with RS facing and A, pick up and k28 sts along one side edge of the 29 rows of chart patt.
**Next row:** Purl.
**Next row:** K1 *yf, k2tog; rep from * to last st, k1.
**Next row:** Purl.
Work a further 2 rows in st st, then cast off.
Work other side edge similarly.

### Front band edgings

Work as for collar edgings, picking up 28 sts along side edge of each front band at hem.

Tidy loose ends back into own colours. Press pieces lightly on WS. Place markers 7½[8:8½]in (19[20.5:21.5]cm) down from shoulder seam at back and fronts. Sew cast-on edge of sleeve between markers. Join side and sleeve seams. Fold back facings at picot line and hem in place on sleeves, hem, bands and collar. Similarly, fold back collar and front band edgings and stitch in place. Steam seams, hems, bands and collar.

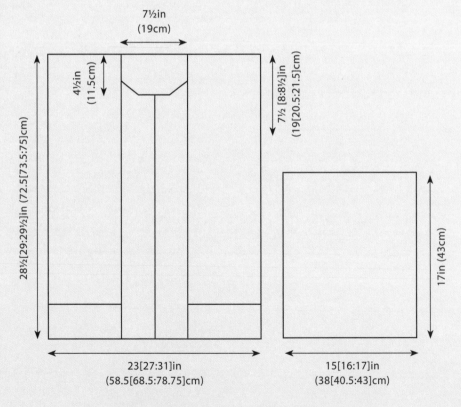

# Oriental flowers chart (100 sts x 88 rows)

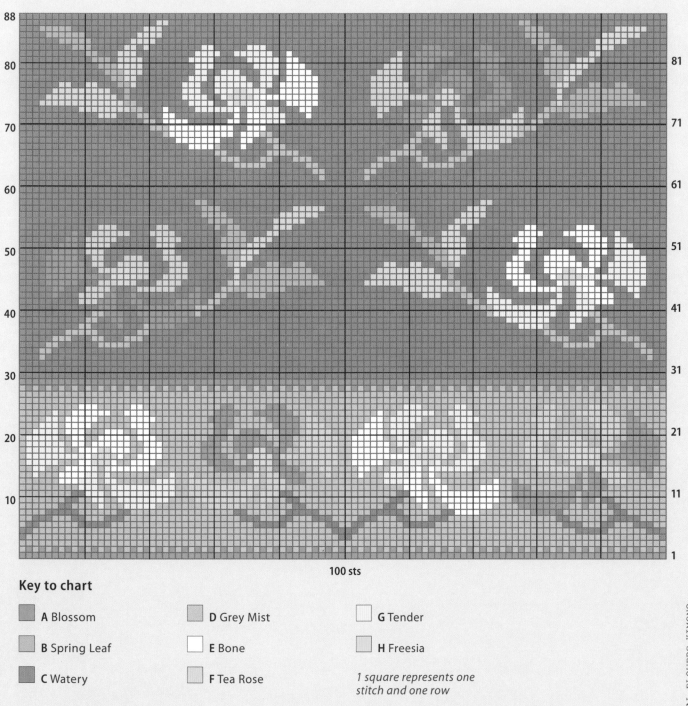

100 sts

## Key to chart

| | | |
|---|---|---|
| **A** Blossom | **D** Grey Mist | **G** Tender |
| **B** Spring Leaf | **E** Bone | **H** Freesia |
| **C** Watery | **F** Tea Rose | *1 square represents one stitch and one row* |

Sasha and the Rowan story

# Yarn matters

**KATE BULLER**, SENIOR BRAND MANAGER FOR ROWAN YARNS, LOOKS BACK OVER THE LAST 30 YEARS AT HOW ROWAN AND SASHA HAVE WORKED TOGETHER TO PRODUCE SOME TIMELESS DESIGNS

**Above:** The front cover of Rowan Book 1, 1986.

**Left:** A selection of vintage Rowan shade cards.

Sasha Kagan's collaboration with Rowan dates back to a serendipitous meeting with its founder Stephen Sheard, in 1984 at a trade show in Brighton, where Rowan was showing one of its first collections of hand-knit yarn. Stephen recognized that Sasha's designs could be very much at the heart of Rowan's philosophy. He says, 'The British Designer Knitters were a phenomena of the great push for freedom, creativity and expression of our generation [the 1960s]. We wanted to build an alternative life away from big business, back to a gentler way of living based on creativity and designer artisans. Sasha was in the vanguard of this movement five decades ago.'

At that time, Sasha had been prompted by enthusiastic feedback from knitters to publish a book featuring multiple-size classic shapes for the whole family, following the success of *The Sasha Kagan Sweater Book* (Dorling Kindersley, 1984), which primarily featured Shetland 4-ply wool. As a result of the meeting with Stephen, she decided to choose Rowan yarn for her second book *Big and Little Sweaters* (Dorling Kindersley, 1987). Using Rowan's 4-ply Botany as a solid colour, in contrast to the 1950s-feel flecked backgrounds, enabled Sasha to give a sharp graphic quality to her designs.

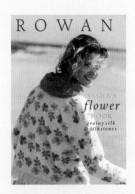

**Above:** Front cover of *Sasha's Flower Book*, 1989.

Alongside her new book, Sasha was commissioned by Rowan to design the 'Under/Over' sweater for Rowan book 1 – a classic Memphis-inspired colour statement. Another commission soon followed for Rowan book 2 ('Vinca'). From the use of grainy silks and silkstones in this design, *Sasha's Flower Book* was born, a Rowan publication containing nine sophisticated, luxury womenswear pieces. This collection explored the use of soft, feminine colours and textures using the silk blends for backgrounds, fine cotton chenille for velvets and mulberry silk for reflective surfaces.

The relationship between Sasha and Rowan now cemented, she went on to contribute to many of its magazines and books over the years. We cannot discuss every design, but some of the most memorable ones are mentioned here.

For Rowan Book 10, the famous Swallows and Amazons collection, Sasha came up with 'Hawthorn'. This William Morris-inspired piece was later reworked in Magpie Aran and Chunky Cotton Chenille as a coat for the Victoria and Albert Museum. Demand for big statement pieces continued and Rowan Book 16's 'October Leaf' is a good example of a simple mirror image print brought to life with the rich velvety texture of Chunky Cotton Chenille knitted on a Magpie Aran background.

In 2000, Sasha had a landmark show at the Victoria and Albert Museum celebrating 10 years' worth of designs using Rowan's finest yarns. Sasha exhibited a collection of hand-knit pieces at the show and also published her third book *Country Inspiration* (Taunton, 2000) to coincide with the occasion. The exhibition continued in Japan the following year with the Mitsukoshi British Fair. The influence of Japanese patterning can be seen in Rowan book 32 'Snowberry' using Rowanspun 4-ply and DK. Floral sprays decorate the yoke balanced by a tiny border at cuff and welts. The relaxed twist of this 100% wool quality provided a perfect foil for the elegant berry branches.

**Top:** 'Triangle' from *Vogue Knitting*, 1986, uses Rowan Fleck DK Tweed.

**Bottom:** 'Tiny Flower' from the *A Yorkshire Fable* book.

One of the recurring themes in Sasha's work is mixing together geometric texture and intarsia motifs, which enables the design to work on two different levels. In Rowan Book 33 Sasha used this technique with fine 4-ply cotton to create 'Diagonal Flowers', a classic navy sweater with diamond ribs mirroring at centre back, front and sleeves.

2003 saw the introduction of Yorkshire Tweed and *A Yorkshire Fable* book of designs. Sasha came up with two clever designs to emphasize the delicate nature of this lovely fibre. 'Cable Rose', was a chequer board pattern of cables and roses and 'Tiny Flower' used a vertical play of random cables and minute flowers.

**Above:** 'Under/Over' design from Rowan Book 1, 1986.

The first example of vertical panels of lace and motifs used together appeared in Rowan Book 34 as 'Rosebud'. Rowan's 50% wool 50% cotton was ideal for this design as it relied on stitch definition for the full effect. It also worked beautifully for 'Diamond Leaf', which explored a self-coloured lattice pattern with leaves worked in Summer Tweed and Chunky Chenille.

In 2004, feeling the need to encourage the next generation to pick up yarn and needles, Sasha authored her first 'how to' book *Knitting for Beginners* (Carroll & Brown, 2004). Rowan's Big Wool and Polar were ideal for this publication, which offered patterns that could be finished in hours. In the same year Rowan ran a vintage 1970s story in its Book 36, and Sasha contributed 'Daisy', a homage to Mary Quant's famous logo, Ossie Clark's sharp tailoring and a nostalgic reminder of student days spent on the Kings Road.

Scottish Tweed was another of Sasha's favourites and she used Rowan's cleverly blended Shetland Wool in 'Scottish Island Knits' and her next book *Knitwear* (GMC Publications, 2008). The Harlequin leaf coat is a good example. The possibility of using two ends of 4-ply to make a DK weight enlarged the colour palette, which, for a designer like Sasha who sees yarn as paint, opened up fantastic opportunities. The blending of colours in the Tapestry range of long print soya protein and wool provided a vehicle for 'Pebble' and 'Laurel', and Rowan's Summer Tweed gave the required desert feel for 'Baluchistan Stripe'.

Rowan's 30th anniversary in 2008 was celebrated with the publication of Magazine 44, which showcased seven designers, including Sasha and her signature design, 'Rosebud'. It was re-knitted and coloured in Felted Tweed and Wool cotton and modelled by Sasha herself in the Yorkshire Dales. To celebrate, Rowan also launched an exhibition that travelled all over the world showing the very best of Rowan over the last three decades. The important part that Sasha has played in Rowan's achievement was recognized in the exhibition along with other renowned designers such as Kaffe Fassett, Jean Moss and Kim Hargreaves. As Stephen Sheard says: 'Today she is one of the very few still expressing their distinct personality through their design and their craft. Kaffe Fassett and Marion Foale are two others in this, now rare, pantheon. It has been a great privilege to have worked over so many years with Sasha and been inspired by her design integrity.'

Sasha remains one of Rowan's favourite designers and *The Classic Collection* sees garments from four decades reworked in today's softer, more luxurious yarns: Kid Silk Aura for Sweet William, Silky Tweed for Tulip and Baby Alpaca DK mixed with pure silk for Oriental Flowers.

**Below:** 'Rosebud' is the first design to show vertical panels and motifs used together.

YARN MATTERS

'SOFT, LUXURIOUS ECO-FIBRES EMPHASIZED DRAPE
AND MOVEMENT – ETHICS, FAIR TRADE AND THE HAND
KNIT AS ART FORM, COMBINED WITH VINTAGE DESIGNS
AND THE FASHION CLOCK BEGAN AGAIN.'

2000–09

Originally a wraparound coat
designed in 1996 for Henri Bendel's
'Inspirations: The British Hand
knitters' exhibition in New York,
Ivy is still popular across the decades
as an all-time country classic.

# Ivy hooded coat

## Sizes
XS[S:M:L:XL]
**To fit bust**
34[36:38:40:42]in
(86[91:96:101:106]cm)
**Actual measurements**
44[46:48:50:52]in
(112[117:122:127:132]cm)
**Length**
31½[31½:32:32½:32½]in
(80[80:81.25:82.5:82.5]cm)
**Sleeve seam**
18in (45.75cm)
Figures in square brackets refer to
larger sizes: where there is only one
set of figures this applies to all sizes.

## You will need
Jamieson & Smith Shetland wool 2-ply
jumper weight (knits as 4-ply)
(129yds/118m per 25g ball)
13[14:14:15:15] balls **292 Oat (A)**
3[4:4:4:4] balls FC12 **Olive Mix (F)**
2 balls FC50 **Dusky Rose (B)**
2 balls 72 **Terracotta (C)**
2 balls 118 **Mistletoe Green (E)**
2 balls 133 **Wine (G)**
2 balls FC38 **Bracken (I)**
1[1:1:2:2] balls **134 Grape (D)**
1[1:1:2:2] balls 9113 **Lacquer (H)**
1 ball FC56 **Blue Wine Mix (J)**
1 pair each of 3.25mm (US3:UK10)
and 3.75mm (US5:UK9) needles
Stitch markers
7 x ¾in (20mm) buttons

## Tension
26 sts and 30 rows to 4in(10cm) over
chart pattern.
*Use larger or smaller needles if
necessary to obtain correct tension.*

## Pattern notes
This design uses the intarsia woven
method, see page 155.

## Back

Using 3.25mm needles and A cast on 144[150:156:162:170] sts and work 6 rows in st st.

**Next row (picot):** K1, *yo, K2tog; rep from * to last st, k1.

Work 7 rows st st.

Change to 3.75mm needles, refer to chart and work the 121 rows, rep from row 22 to end. Centre chart as foll: Work the last 42[45:48:51:55] sts of chart, work the 60 sts of chart, work the first 42[45:48:51:55] sts.

Cont in patt as set until work measures 22[22:22¼:22½:22½]in (56[56:56.5:57:57]cm) from picot fold line, ending on WS row.

### Shape armholes

Cast off 7 sts at beg of next 2 rows (130[136:142:148:156] sts).

Cont in patt as set until work measures 30½[30½:31:31½:31½]in (77.5[77.5:78.75:80:80]cm) from picot fold line, ending on WS row.

### Shape shoulders

Cast off 14[15:16:17:18] sts at beg of next 2 rows.

Cast off 15[16:16:17:18] sts at beg of foll 4 rows. Cast off rem 42[42:46:46:48] sts.

## Left front

Using 3.25mm needles and A cast on 72[74:78:80:84] sts and work 6 rows in st st.

**Next row (picot):** K1, *yo, K2tog; rep from * to last st, k1.

Work 7 rows st st.

Change to 3.75mm needles and refer to chart and work the 121 rows, rep from row 22 to end. Centre chart as foll:

**RS rows:** Work the last 42[45:48:51:55] sts of chart, work first 30[29:30:29:29] sts.

**WS rows:** Work the last 30[29:30:29:29] sts of chart, work first 42[45:48:51:55] sts.

Cont in patt as set until work measures 22[22:22¼:22½:22½]in

(56[56:56.5:57:57]cm) from picot fold line, ending on WS row.

### Shape armhole

Cast off 7 sts at beg of next row.

Cont in patt as set until work measures 27½[27½:28:28½:28½]in (70[70:71:72.5:72.5]cm) from picot fold line, ending on RS row.

### Shape neck

Cast off 6 sts at beg of next row.

Work 1 row.

Dec 1 st at beg of next and every foll row 12[12:16:16:18] times, then on every foll alt row 3[3:1:1:0] times (44[47:48:51:54] sts).

Cont in patt as set until work measures 30¾[30¾:31¼:31¾:31¾]in (78[78:79.5:80.75:80.75]cm) from picot fold line, ending on WS row.

### Shape shoulders

Cast off 14[15:16:17:18] sts at beg of next row. Work 1 row.

Cast off 15[16:16:17:18] sts at beg of next and foll alt row.

## Right front

Work as for left front, reversing all shapings. Centre chart as foll:

**RS rows:** Work the last 30[29:30:29:29] sts of chart, work first 42[45:48:51:55] sts.

**WS rows:** Work the last 42[45:48:51:55] sts of chart, work first 30[29:30:29:29] sts.

## Sleeves

Using 3.25mm needles and F cast on 60[60:64:66:66] sts. Work 4in(10cm) in k1, p1 twisted rib in the following stripe sequence, carrying unused yarn up sides of work:

**Row 1:** I

**Row 2:** G

**Row 3:** F

Change to 3.75mm needles and refer to chart, centring it as foll: Work the last 0[0:0:3:3] sts, work the 60 sts of chart, work the first 0[0:0:3:3] sts. At the same time inc 1 st at both

ends of the next and every foll alt row 5 times, then every 4th row 20 times (taking extra sts into patt as they occur) (110[110:114:116:116] sts). Cont in patt as set until sleeve measures 19in (48.25cm) from cast-on edge and then cast off.

## Hood

Using 3.25mm needles and F cast on 172[172:176:176:180] sts.

Work 6 rows in k1, p1 twisted rib stripe sequence as for cuffs.

Change to 3.75mm needles and refer to chart and work 8 rows, centring chart as foll:

Work the last 56[56:58:58:0] sts, work the 60 sts 1[1:1:1:3] times, work first 56[56:58:58:0] sts.

### Begin hood shaping

Dec 1 st at both ends of next and every foll 3rd row until there are 158[158:162:162:166] sts, then at each end of every foll alt row until 148[148:152:152:156] sts.

Cont in patt as set until hood measures 10½in (27cm) from cast-on edge, then cast off.

## Finishing

Join shoulder seams.

### Right front band

Using 3.25mm needles and F, with RS facing pick up and k1 st for each row evenly along front edge between picot row and beg of neck shaping. Mark position of 7 buttonholes: First hole 5½in (14cm) up from picot row, the last hole 4 sts down from neck shaping, the rest spaced evenly in between. Working in k1, p1 twisted rib in stripe sequence as for cuffs, work 6 rows making 7 buttonholes in rows 3 and 4 by casting off 3 sts at markers and casting on these sts again on foll row. Cast off.

**Left front band**
Work as for right front band omitting buttonholes.

Tidy loose ends back into own colours. Press pieces lightly on WS avoiding ribbing. Sew cast-off edge of sleeve into straight armhole edge. Sew top 1in (2.5cm) of sleeve to cast-off edge of armhole forming a neat right angle. Join side seams and sleeve seams in one line. Fold facings to inside and hem. Join back seam of hood. Attach hood to neck. Sew on buttons opposite buttonholes. Steam seams.

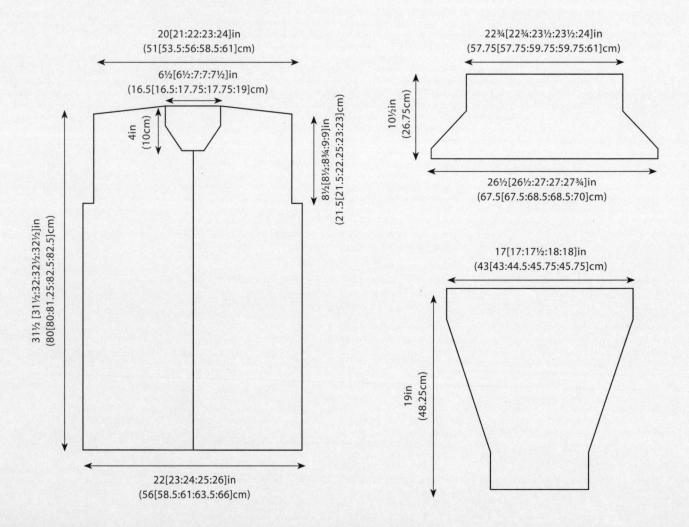

20[21:22:23:24]in
(51[53.5:56:58.5:61]cm)

6½[6½:7:7:7½]in
(16.5[16.5:17.75:17.75:19]cm)

4in
(10cm)

8½[8½:8¾:9:9]in
(21.5[21.5:22.25:23:23]cm)

31½[31½:32:32½:32½]in
(80[80:81.25:82.5:82.5]cm)

22[23:24:25:26]in
(56[58.5:61:63.5:66]cm)

22¾[22¾:23½:23½:24]in
(57.75[57.75:59.75:59.75:61]cm)

10½in
(26.75cm)

26½[26½:27:27:27¾]in
(67.5[67.5:68.5:68.5:70]cm)

17[17:17½:18:18]in
(43[43:44.5:45.75:45.75]cm)

19in
(48.25cm)

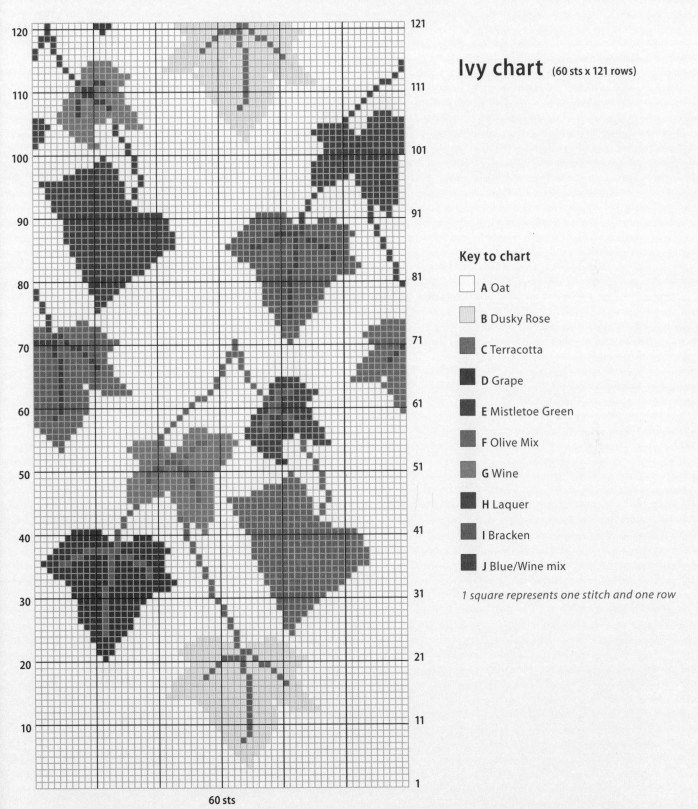

## Ivy chart (60 sts x 121 rows)

### Key to chart

☐ **A** Oat

**B** Dusky Rose

**C** Terracotta

**D** Grape

**E** Mistletoe Green

**F** Olive Mix

**G** Wine

**H** Laquer

**I** Bracken

**J** Blue/Wine mix

*1 square represents one stitch and one row*

60 sts

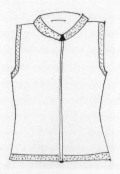

First created for Colinette Yarn's *Secret Garden* pattern book, this elemental floral print tries to capture the feeling of spring with delicate blossoms twisting and turning in the breeze.

# Elderflower body-warmer

## Sizes
XS[S:M:L:XL]
**To fit bust**
34[36:38:40:42]in (86[91:96:101:106]cm)
**Actual measurements**
34[36:38:40:42]in (86[91:96:101:106]cm)
**Length**
24[24:24½:25:25]in
(61[61:62.25:63.5:63.5]cm)
*Figures in square brackets refer to larger sizes: where there is only one set of figures this applies to all sizes.*

## You will need
Rowan Felted Tweed Aran
(95yds/87m per 50g ball)
7[7:7:8:8] balls 730 **Stormy Blue (A)**
1 ball 722 **Burnt (B)**
Rowan Felted Tweed DK
(191yds/175m per 50g ball)
1 ball 161 **Avocado (C)**
Rowan Silk DK
(137yds/125m per 50g ball)
2 balls 151 **Bone (D)**
1 ball 156 **Tranquil (E)**
Rowan Cashsoft DK
(126yds/115m per 50g ball)
1[1:1:2:2] balls 509 **Lime (F)**
Rowan Wool Cotton
(123yds/113m per 50g ball)
1 ball 974 **Freesia (G)**
1 pair each of 3.25mm (US3:UK10)

and 4mm (US6:UK8) needles
zip to fit approximately
20½[20½:21:21½:21½]in
(52[52:53.5:54.75:54.75]cm)
Stitch holders

## Tension
20 sts and 26 rows to 4in (10cm)
over chart patt using 4mm needles.
*Use larger or smaller needles if necessary to obtain correct tension.*

## Pattern notes
This design uses the intarsia woven method, see page 155.

## Back

Using 3.25mm needles and A cast on 88[92:98:102:108] sts. Work 1in (2.5cm) in moss st ending on WS row. Change to 4mm needles and refer to chart and rep the 88 rows to end of work, centring chart as foll:

Work last 0[2:5:7:10] sts, work the 44 sts of chart twice, work the first 0[2:5:7:10] sts.

When work measures 2in (5cm) from cast-on edge ending on WS row, commence shaping.

### Shape sides

Keeping patt correct as set, dec as foll:

**XS:** Dec 1 st at both ends of next and every foll 6th row 7 times (74 sts).

**S:** Dec 1 st at both ends of next, then every foll 4th row twice, then every foll 6th row 5 times (76 sts).

**M:** Dec 1 st at both ends of next, then every foll 4th row 6 times, then every foll 6th row 3 times (78 sts).

**L:** Dec 1 st at both ends of next, then every foll 4th row 7 times, then every foll 6th row 3 times (80 sts).

**XL:** Dec 1 st at both ends of next, then every alt row once, then every foll 4th row 11 times (82 sts).

Work 11[9:9:9:9] rows in patt without shaping.

Then inc, incorporating extra sts into patt, as foll:

**XS:** Inc 1 st at both ends of next and every foll 6th row twice, then every 8th row 3 times (86 sts).

**S:** Inc 1 st at both ends of next, then every foll 4th row once, then every foll 6th row 5 times (90 sts).

**M:** Inc 1 st at both ends of next, then every foll 4th row 8 times (96 sts).

**L:** Inc 1 st at both ends of next, then every alt row 3 times, then every 4th row 6 times (100 sts).

**XL:** Inc 1 st at both ends of next, then every alt row 8 times, then every 4th row 3 times (106 sts).

Cont in patt as set until back measures 16[15¾:16:16¼:16]in (40.75[40:40.75:41.25:40.75]cm) from cast-on edge ending on WS row.

### Shape armholes

Cast off 4[4:5:5:5] sts of beg of next 2 rows. Then dec 1 st at both ends of next and every foll alt row 7[8:9:10:13] times (64[66:68:70:70] sts).

Cont in patt as set until work measures 23[23:23½:24:24]in (58.5[58.5:59.75:61:61]cm) from cast-on edge ending on WS row.

### Shape shoulders

Cast off 5 sts at beg of next 2 rows.
Cast off 5[5:6:6:6] sts at beg of next 2 rows.
Cast off 6 sts at beg of next 2 rows.
Leave rem 32[34:34:36:36] sts on holder.

## Left front

Using 3.25mm needles and A cast on 44[46:49:51:54] sts.

Work 1in(2.5cm) in moss st ending on WS row.

Change to 4mm needles and refer to chart and rep the 88 rows to end of work, centring chart as foll:

**RS rows:** Work last 0[2:5:7:10] sts, work the 44 sts of chart.

**WS rows:** Work 44 sts of chart, then work first 0[2:5:7:10] sts.

When work measures 2in (5cm) from cast-on edge ending on WS row, commence shaping.

### Shape side

Keeping patt correct as set, dec as foll:

**XS:** Dec 1 st at beg of next and every foll 6th row 7 times (37 sts).

**S:** Dec 1 st at beg of next, then every foll 4th row twice, then every foll 6th row 5 times (38 sts).

**M:** Dec 1 st at beg of next, then every foll 4th row 6 times, then every foll 6th row 3 times (39 sts).

**L:** Dec 1 st at beg of next, then every

foll 4th row 7 times, then every foll 6th row 3 times (40 sts).

**XL:** Dec 1 st at beg of next, then every alt row once, then every foll 4th row 11 times (41 sts).

Work 11[9:9:9:9] rows in patt without shaping.

Then inc, incorporating extra sts into patt, as foll:

**XS:** Inc 1 st at beg of next, then every foll 6th row twice, then every 8th row 3 times (43 sts).

**S:** Inc 1 st at both ends of next, then every foll 4th row once, then every foll 6th row 5 times (45 sts).

**M:** Inc 1 st at both ends of next, then every foll 4th row 8 times (48 sts).

**L:** Inc 1 st at both ends of next, then every alt row 3 times, then every 4th row 6 times (50 sts).

**XL:** Inc 1 st at both ends of next, then every alt row 8 times, then every 4th row 3 times (53 sts).

Cont in patt as set until back measures 16[15¾:16:16¼:16]in (40.75[40:40.75:41.25:40.75]cm) from cast-on edge ending on WS row.

### Shape armhole

Cast off 4[4:5:5:5] sts of beg of next row. Work 1 row. Then dec 1 st at both ends of next and every foll alt row 7[8:9:10:13] times (32[33:34:35:35] sts).

Cont until work measures 20[20:20½:21:21]in (51[51:52:53.5:53.5]cm) from cast-on edge, end on RS row.

### Shape neck

Place 5 sts on holder at beg of next row. Then dec 1 st at neck edge on next and every foll row 11[12:12:13:13] times (16[16:17:17:17] sts).

Cont in patt as set until work measures 23[23:23½:24:24]in (58.5[58.5:59.75:61:61]cm) from cast-on edge ending on WS row.

### Shape shoulders

Cast off 5 sts at beg of next row.
Work 1 row.
Cast off 5[5:6:6:6] sts at beg of next row. Work 1 row.
Cast off rem 6 sts.

### Right front

Work as for left front reversing all shapings. Centre chart as foll:
**RS rows:** Work the 44 sts of chart, work the first 0[2:5:7:10] sts.
**WS rows:** Work the last 0[2:5:7:10] sts, work the 44 sts of chart.

### Finishing

#### Left front band

Using 3.25mm needles and A, with RS facing pick up and k 114[114:118:120:120] sts from neck shaping to welt. Work 4 rows moss st. Cast off in moss st.

#### Right front band

Work as for left front band picking up sts from welt to neck shaping. Join shoulder seams.

#### Armbands

Using 3.25mm needles and A, with RS facing, pick up and k 100[104:108:110:114] sts around armholes. Work 1in (2.5cm) in moss st, dec 1 st at both ends of every alt row. Cast off in moss st.

### Neckband

Using 3.25mm needles and A, with RS facing, pick up and k 3 sts along top of right band, k across 5 sts on holder at right front neck, pick up and k 26 sts along right neck edge, k across 32[34:34:36:36] sts on holder at centre back, pick up and k 26 sts along left neck edge, k across 5 sts on holder at left front neck and pick up and k 3 sts along top of left band (100[100:102:104:104] sts).

Work 1in (2.5cm) in moss st.
Cast off in moss st.

Tidy loose ends back into own colours. Press pieces on WS avoiding welts. Join side and armband seams. Sew in zip. Steam seams.

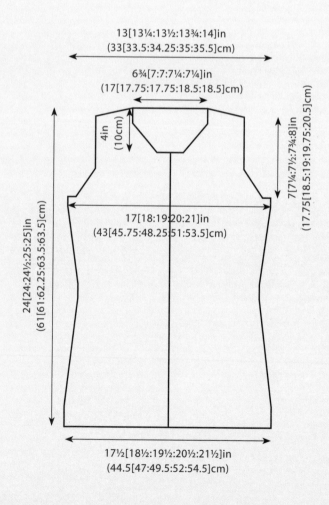

13[13¼:13½:13¾:14]in
(33[33.5:34.25:35:35.5]cm)

6¾[7:7:7¼:7¼]in
(17[17.75:17.75:18.5:18.5]cm)

4in
(10cm)

7[7¼:7½:7¾:8]in
(17.75[18.5:19:19.75:20.5]cm)

17[18:19:20:21]in
(43[45.75:48.25:51:53.5]cm)

24[24:24½:25:25]in
(61[61:62.25:63.5:63.5]cm)

17½[18½:19½:20½:21½]in
(44.5[47:49.5:52:54.5]cm)

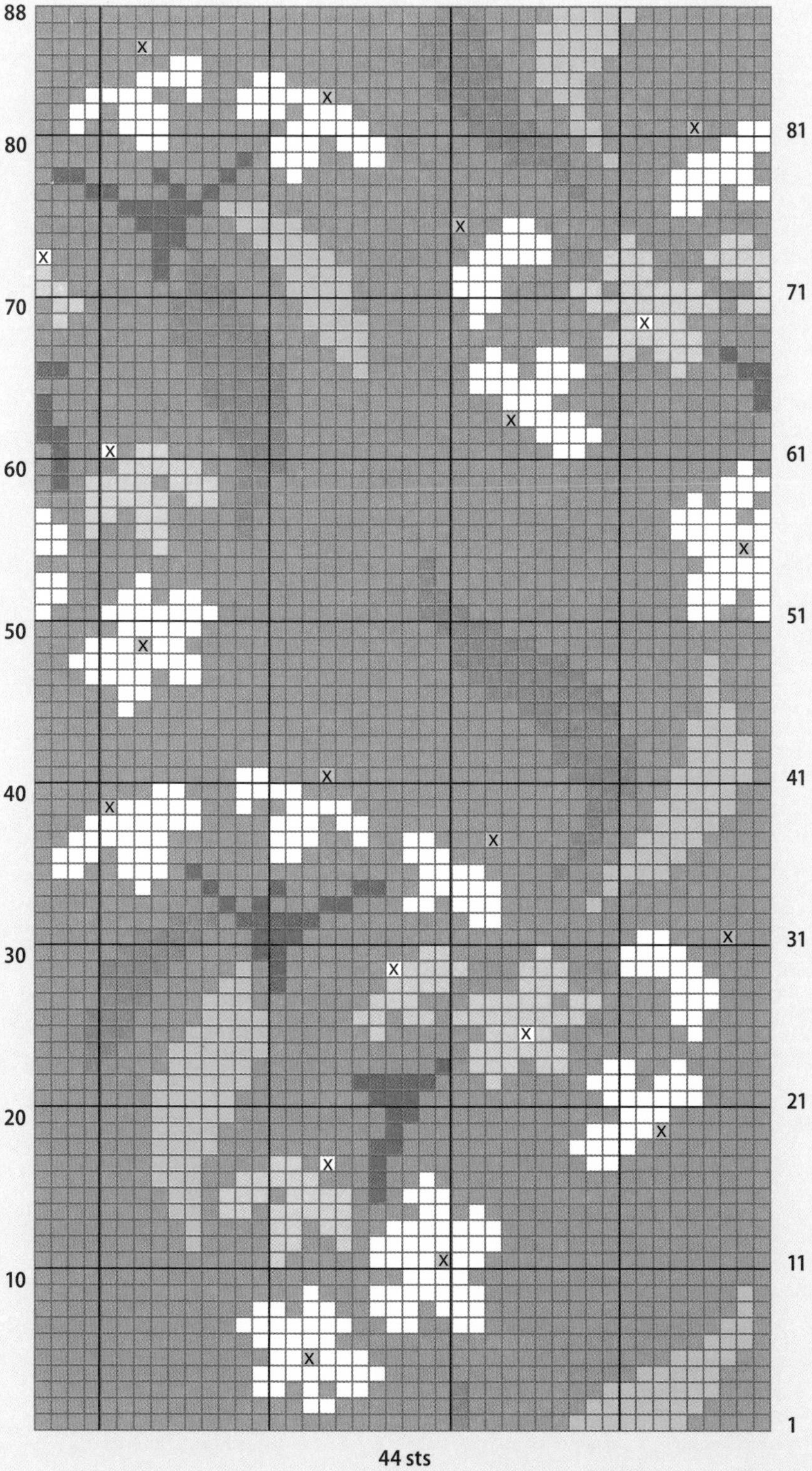

## Elderflower chart
**(44 sts x 88 rows)**

### Key to chart

A Storm Blue

B Burnt

C Avocado

D Bone

E Tranquil

F Lime

G Freesia

X Bobble in D

X Bobble in G

*1 square represents one stitch and one row*

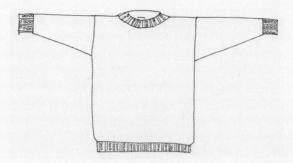

Plants are a constant delight to me and so is the birth of a new flower design. Originally created as a 1920's-inspired flapper jacket in *Country Inspiration*, 2000, this design is now a casual sloppy joe.

# Sweet William sloppy joe

## Sizes
XS[S:M:L:XL]
**To fit bust**
34[36:38:40:42]in (86[91:96:101:106]cm)
**Actual measurements**
44[46:48:50:52]in
(112[117:122:127:132]cm)
**Length**
28[28:29:29:30]in
(71[71:73.75:73.75:76.25]cm)
**Sleeve seams**
18in (46cm)
*Figures in square brackets refer to larger sizes; where there is only one set of figures this applies to all sizes.*

## You will need
Rowan Kid Silk Aura
(82yds/75m per 25g ball)
13[14:15:15:16] balls 750 **Ivory (A)**
Rowan Kid Classic
(153yds/140m per 50g ball)
1 ball 870 **Rosewood (B)**
1 ball 854 **Tea Rose (C)**
1 ball 835 **Royal (D)**
1 ball 863 **Lipstick (E)**
1 ball 847 **Cherry Red (F)**
1 ball 852 **Victoria (G)**
1 ball 853 **Spruce (H)**
Rowan Kid Silk Haze
(229yds/210m) per 25g ball)
*NB: use this yarn triple throughout*
1 ball 644 **Ember (I)**
1 ball 579 **Splendour (J)**

Rowan Felted Tweed
(191yds/175m per 50g ball)
1 ball 161 **Avocado (K)**
1 pair each of 3mm (US3:UK11) and
3.75mm (US5:UK9) needles
Stitch holder and markers

## Tension
26 sts and 29 rows to 4in (10cm) over chart pattern.
*Use larger or smaller needles if necessary to obtain correct tension.*

## Pattern notes

This design uses the intarsia woven method, see page 155.

**Bobble rib** (multiple of 9 sts)

**Row 1(RS):** K1, p3, k1, p3, k1.

**Row 2:** P1, k3, p1, k3, p1.

**Row 3:** K1, p3, (k1, yo, k1) into same st, turn, p1, p1tbl, p1, turn, k into front and back of all 3 sts, do NOT turn, pass all sts, one at a time, over last st.

## Back

Using 3mm needles and A cast on 144[144:153:162:162] sts. Work 1½in (4cm) in bobble rib, ending on WS row and inc 0[6:3:0:8] sts evenly across final row (144[150:156:162:170] sts).

Change to 3.75mm needles and refer to chart and work the 90 rows twice (180 rows).

Centre chart as foll:

Work 2[5:8:11:15] sts in st st in A, work 70 sts of chart twice, work 2[5:8:11:15] sts in st st in A (144[150:156:162:170] sts).

*NB: for all sizes, when 180 rows of chart are completed, cont in A in st st to end.*

Cont until work measures 27[27:28:28:29]in (68.5[68.5:71:71:73.75]cm) from cast-on edge ending on WS row.

### Shape shoulders

Cast off 15[16:17:17:19] sts at beg of next 2 rows.

Cast off 15[16:17:18:19] sts at beg of foll 2 rows.

Cast off 16[17:18:18:19] sts at beg of foll 2 rows.

Cast off rem 52[52:52:56:56] sts.

## Front

Work as for back until work measures 24[24:25:25:26]in (61[61:63.5:63.5:66]cm) from cast-on edge ending on WS row.

### Shape neck

With RS facing, work 67[70:73:74:78] sts, turn. Working on these 67[70:73:74:78] sts only dec 1 st at neck edge on every row until 46[49:52:53:57] sts rem.

Cont straight until front work measures 27[27:28:28:29]in (68.5[68.5:71:71:73.75]cm) from cast-on edge ending on WS row.

### Shape shoulder

Cast off 15[16:17:17:19] sts at beg of next row. Work 1 row.

Cast off 15[16:17:18:19] sts at beg of next row. Work 1 row.

Cast off rem 16[17:18:18:19] sts at beg of next row.

With RS facing, place first 10[10:10:14:14] sts onto a st holder, rejoin yarn to rem sts and complete as for left side, working shapings on WS rows.

## Sleeves

Using 3mm needle and A cast on 63[63:63:70:70] sts. Work 3in (7.75cm) in bobble rib, dec 1 st on last row for XS, S and M sizes (62[62, 62, 70, 70] sts).

Change to 3.75mm needles and work the 90 rows.

*NB: for XS, S, and M sizes, start on st 5 and end on st 66, incorporating the extra sts as you increase.*

At the same time, work inc as foll:

**XS, S and M:** 1 st at both ends of next and every foll 3rd row 34 times (130 sts).

**L and XL:** 1 st at both ends of next and every foll 3rd row 33 times (136 sts).

*NB: the increased sts are worked in A in st st.*

Cont straight in st st with yarn A until sleeve measures 18in (45.75cm).

Cast off.

## Finishing

### Neckband

Join right shoulder seam.

Using 3mm needles and with RS facing join A at left front shoulder, pick up and k29 sts down left neck shaping, k across 10[10:10:14:14] sts on holder at centre front, pick up and k29 sts up right neck shaping and 49[49:49:54:54] sts from back neck (117[117:117:126:126] sts).

Starting on row 2 (WS) work 11 rows in bobble pattern, then cast off in rib.

Tidy loose ends back into own colours. Steam pieces gently on WS avoiding ribbing. Place markers 10[10:10:10½:10½]in (25.5[25.5:25.5:26.75:26.75]cm) down from shoulder seams. Sew top of sleeves between markers. Join side seams and sleeve seams in one line. Join neckband. Steam seams.

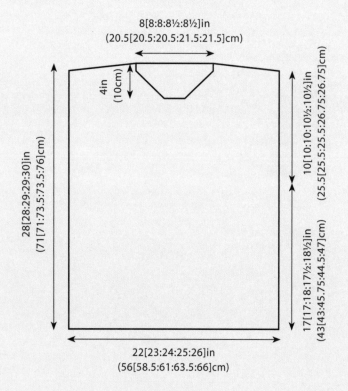

8[8:8:8½:8½]in
(20.5[20.5:20.5:21.5:21.5]cm)

4in
(10cm)

28[28:29:29:30]in
(71[71:73.5:73.5:76]cm)

10[10:10:10½:10½]in
(25.5[25.5:25.5:26.75:26.75]cm)

17[17:18:17½:18½]in
(43[43:45.75:44.5:47]cm)

22[23:24:25:26]in
(56[58.5:61:63.5:66]cm)

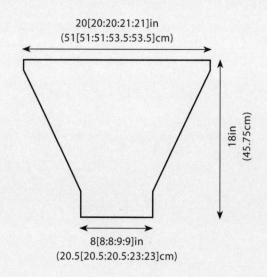

20[20:20:21:21]in
(51[51:51:53.5:53.5]cm)

18in
(45.75cm)

8[8:8:9:9]in
(20.5[20.5:20.5:23:23]cm)

# Sweet William chart (70 sts x 90 rows)

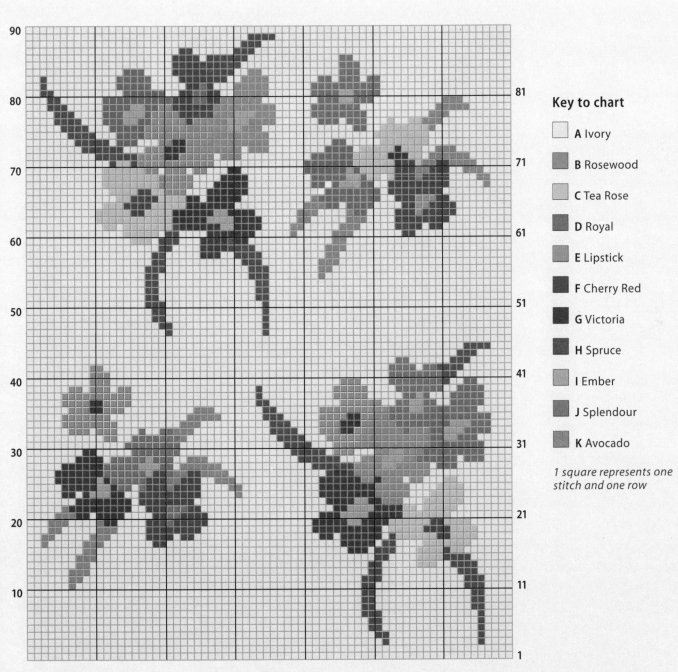

**Key to chart**

| | A Ivory |
|---|---|
| | B Rosewood |
| | C Tea Rose |
| | D Royal |
| | E Lipstick |
| | F Cherry Red |
| | G Victoria |
| | H Spruce |
| | I Ember |
| | J Splendour |
| | K Avocado |

*1 square represents one stitch and one row*

First commissioned in 2008 by *The Knitter* magazine for a folklore fusion story, I created this design. It is a mixture of Mid-European stylized flower and heart motifs blended with a Nordic spot pattern.

# Carinthia tunic

## Sizes
XS[S:M:L:XL]
**To fit bust**
34[36:38:40:42]in
(86[91:96:101:106]cm)
**Actual measurements**
25[27:29:31:33]in
(63.5[68.5:73.5:78.5:83.5]cm) when unstretched
**Length**
29½[29½:30:30:30½]in
(75[75:76.25:76.25:77.5]cm)
*Figures in square brackets refer to larger sizes; where there is only one set of figures this applies to all sizes.*

## You will need
UK Alpaca DK
(166yds/152m per 50g ball)
8[8:8:9:9] balls 06 **Black (A)**
2 balls 13 **Wine (B)**
1 ball 09 **Mustard (C)**
1 ball 20 **Bluebell (D)**
1 ball 15 **Rust (E)**
1 ball 07 **Jade (F)**
1 ball 03 **Fawn (G)**
1 pair each of 2.75mm (US2:UK12), 3mm (US3:UK11) and 3.75mm (US5:UK9) needles
Stitch holder

## Tension
24 sts and 34 rows to 4in (10cm) over chart pattern.
35 sts and 34 rows to 4in (10cm) over twisted rib.
*Use larger or smaller needles if necessary to obtain correct tension.*

## Pattern notes
This design uses the intarsia woven method, see page 155.

## Back

Using 3mm needles and A cast on 142[148:154:160:166] sts and work 6 rows in moss st.

Change to 3.75mm needles and refer to chart and work the 64 rows, then rep rows 55–64 to end.

Centre chart as foll:

Work the last 57[0:3:6:9] sts of chart, work the 60 sts of chart 1[2:2:2:2] times, work the first 25[28:31:34:37] sts. At the same time dec 1 st at beg and end of 19th and following 18th rows until 130[136:142:148:154] sts rem. Cont in patt as set until back measures 17in (43cm) from cast-on edge ending on WS row.

**Next row:** Change to 2.75mm needles and using A only *k4[5:6:7:8], k2tog; rep from * to last 4[3:6:4:4] sts, k4[3:6:4:4] sts (109[117:125:132:139] sts).

### Back yoke

Working in k1, p1 twisted rib to end, cont until work measures 21½in (54.5cm) from cast-on edge, ending with a WS row.

## Shape armholes

Cast off 7 sts at beg of next 2 rows. Then dec 1 st at both ends of ev alt row 9[12:15:17:19] times (77[79:81:84:87] sts).

Cont as set until work measures 26½[26½:27:27:27½]in (67.5[67.5:68.5:68.5:70]cm) from cast-on edge, ending on WS row.

### Shape neck

Work 29[30:30:31:32] sts and place on hold. Join second ball of yarn and cast off 19[19:21:22:23] sts, work 29[30:30:31:32] sts.

Working both sets of sts at same time, work 1 row, then cont as set, dec 1 st at neck edge every alt row 20 times (9[10:10:11:12] sts).

Work 3 more rows, then cast off.

## Front

Work as for back until work measures 25[25:25½:25½:26]in (63.5[63.5:64.75:64.75:66]cm) from cast-on edge, ending on WS row, centring chart as foll:

Work the last 28[31:34:37:40] sts of chart, work the 60 sts of chart 1[1:2:2:2] times, work the first 54[57:0:3:6] sts.

### Shape neck

Work 24[25:25:26:27] sts and place on a holder. Join in a second ball of yarn and cast off 29[29:31:32:33] sts, work 24[25:25:26:27] sts.

Working both sets of sts at same time, work 1 row, then cont as set, dec 1 st at neck edge every alt row 15 times (9[10:10:11:12] sts).

Work 7 more rows, then cast off.

## Finishing

Tidy loose ends back into own colours. Press pieces lightly on WS avoiding ribbing. Join side seams and shoulder seams. Steam seams. Make a 70[72:74:76:78]in (178[183:188:193:198]cm) twisted cord with A and thread through base of yoke. Make two 1½in (4cm) pompoms with F and attach to each end of cord.

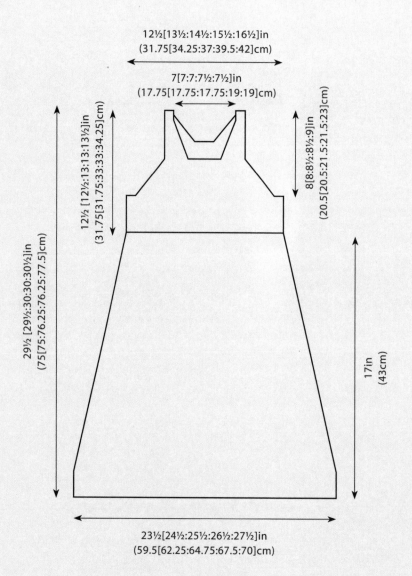

12½[13½:14½:15½:16½]in
(31.75[34.25:37:39.5:42]cm)

7[7:7:7½:7½]in
(17.75[17.75:17.75:19:19]cm)

12½ [12½:13:13:13½]in
(31.75[31.75:33:33:34.25]cm)

8[8½:8½:8½:9]in
(20.5[20.5:21.5:21.5:23]cm)

29½ [29½:30:30:30½]in
(75[75:76.25:76.25:77.5]cm)

17in
(43cm)

23½[24½:25½:26½:27½]in
(59.5[62.25:64.75:67.5:70]cm)

# Carinthia chart (60 sts x 64 rows)

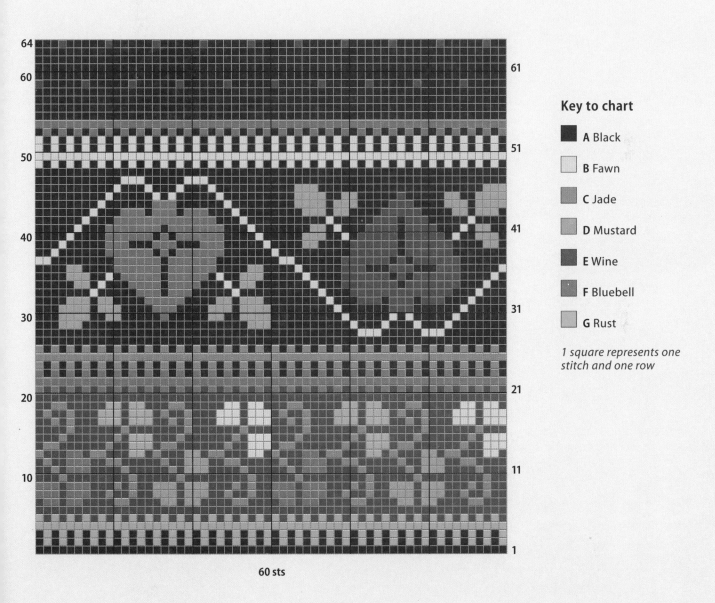

## Key to chart

■ **A** Black

□ **B** Fawn

■ **C** Jade

■ **D** Mustard

■ **E** Wine

■ **F** Bluebell

■ **G** Rust

*1 square represents one stitch and one row*

60 sts

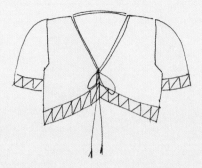

Moving into abstract patterns and exploring the amazing diversity of nature's design repertoire is both a delight and major challenge. 2009 heralds a new and exciting direction for my knitted textiles.

# Lichen bolero

## Sizes
XS[S:M:L:XL]
**To fit bust**
34[36:38:40:42]in (86[91:96:101:106]cm)
**Actual measurements**
34[36:38:40:42]in (86[91:96:101:106]cm)
**Length**
15[15:15½:15½:16]in
(38[38:39.5:39.5:40.75]cm)
**Sleeve seam**
3½in (9cm)
*Figures in square brackets refer to larger sizes; where there is only one set of figures this applies to all sizes.*

## You will need
Rowan Felted Tweed
(191yds/175m per 50g ball)
3 balls 145 **Treacle (A)**
Rowan Kid Classic
(153yds/140m per 50g ball)
1 ball 851 **Straw (B)**
1 ball 852 **Victoria (C)**
1 ball 866 **Bittersweet (D)**
Rowan Cashsoft DK
(126yds/115m per 50g ball)
1 ball 522 **Cashew (E)**
1 ball 533 **Gothic Green (F)**
Rowan Silky Tweed
(137yds/125m per 50g ball)
1 ball 761 **Spinach (G)**
1 ball 751 **Conifer (H)**

3.25mm (US3:UK10) circular needle
1 pair each 3.25mm (US3:UK10) and
4mm (US6:UK8) needles
Stitch markers and holders

## Tension
23 sts and 32 rows to 4in (10cm)
over chart pattern.
*Use larger or smaller needles if necessary to obtain correct tension.*

## Pattern notes

This design uses the intarsia linked method, see page 155.

**Pilsner pleat edging**

Multiple of 8 plus 1

**Row 1(RS):** *K6, k2tog, yo; rep from *, end k1.
**Row 2:** P1, *k1, p7; rep from *.
**Row 3:** *K5, k2tog, yo, p1; rep from *, end k1.
**Row 4:** P1, *k2, p6; rep from *.
**Row 5:** *K4, k2tog, yo, p2; rep from *, end k1.
**Row 6:** P1, *k3, p5; rep from *.
**Row 7:** *K3, k2tog, yo, p3; rep from *, end k1.
**Row 8:** P1, *k4, p4; rep from *.
**Row 9:** *K2, k2tog, yo, p4; rep from *, end k1.
**Row 10:** P1, *k5, p3; rep from *.
**Row 11:** *K1, k2tog, yo, p5; rep from *, end k1.
**Row 12:** P1, *k6, p2; rep from *.
**Row 13:** *K2tog, yo, p6; rep from *, end k1.
**Row 14:** P1, *K7, p1; rep from *.

## Back

Using 3.25mm needles and A cast on 98[104:110:116:122] sts and work 4 rows in garter st.
Change to 4mm needles and refer to chart and rep the 40 rows to end. Centre chart as foll:
**RS rows:** Work 70 sts of chart, then work first 28[34:40:46:52] sts.
**WS rows:** Work last 28[34:40:46:52] sts, then work all 70 sts.
Cont until piece measures 6in (13.5cm) from cast-on edge ending on a WS row.
**Shape armholes**
Cast off 5[5:6:6:6] sts at beg of next 2 rows.
Dec 1 st at both ends of next and foll alt row 5[7:8:10:12] times (78[80:82:84:86] sts).

Cont in patt as set until work measures 14¼[14¼:14¾:14¾:15¼]in (36[36:37.5:37.5:38.75]cm) from cast-on edge, ending on a WS row.
**Shape shoulders**
Cast off 7[8:8:8:8] sts at beg of next 2 rows.
Cast off 8[8:8:8:9] sts at beg of next 2 rows.
Cast off 8[8:9:9:9] sts at beg of next 2 rows.
Cast off rem 32[32:32:34:34] sts.

## Left front

Using 4mm needles and B cast on 2 sts. Refer to chart and start on st 29[35:41:47:53] and work 1 row. Cont with chart, rep the 40 rows to end.
At the same time cast on 5 sts at beg of next and ev alt row 0[2:2:3:3] times, then 4 sts at beg of every foll alt row 5[4:7:8:11] times, then 3 sts at beg of every foll alt row 9[8:5:3:0] times (49[52:55:58:61] sts).
Cont in patt as set until work measures 4[4:4½:4½:5]in (10[10:11.5:11.5:12.75]cm) from cast-on edge, ending on a RS row.
**Shape neck**
Dec 1 st at beg of next and every foll 4th row 16[16:16:17:17] times in all.
**Shape armhole**
At the same time when work measures 6in (13.5cm) from cast-on edge ending on a WS row cast off 5[5:6:6:6] sts at beg of next row. Work 1 row. Then dec 1 st at beg of next and foll alt row 5[7:8:10:12] times (23[24:25:25:26] sts).
Cont in patt as set until work measures 14½[14½:15:15:15½]in (37[37:38:38:39.5]cm) from cast-on edge, ending on a WS row.
**Shape shoulder**
Cast off 7[8:8:8:8] sts at beg of next row. Work 1 row.
Cast off 8[8:8:8:9] sts at beg of next

row. Work 1 row.
Cast off rem 8[8:9:9:9] sts.

## Right front

Work as for left front reversing all shapings, starting chart on st 21[17:15:11:9].

## Sleeves

Using 3.25mm needles and A cast on 78[78:78:84:84] sts and work 4 rows in garter st.
Change to 4mm needles and refer to chart and rep to end, centring chart as foll:
Work the last 4[4:4:7:7] sts, work the 70 sts of chart, work the first 4[4:4:7:7] sts.
Cont in patt as set until work measures 2¼[2¼:2¼:2¾:2¾]in (5.75[5.75:5.75:7:7]cm) from cast-on edge, ending on WS row.
**Shape armhole**
Cast off 5[5:6:6:6] sts at beg of next 2 rows.
Dec 1 st at both ends of every row 2[2:0:0:0] times, then every alt row 20[20:21:23:23] times (24[24:24:26:26] sts).
Work 4 rows in patt as set.
Cast off 3 sts at beg of next 4 rows.
Cast off rem 12[12:12:14:14] sts.

## Finishing

Join shoulder seams and side seams.

**Right front band**

Using 3.25mm needles, with RS facing and A, starting at side seam of right front, pick up and k44[46:50:52:56] sts, place marker A, pick up 4[4:7:7:10] sts along straight front edge, place marker B and pick up and k76 sts up right front neck to shoulder and 16[16:16:17:17] sts to centre back neck (140[142:149:152:159] sts).
Work 4 rows in garter st inc 1 st at markers A and B on rows 2 and 4.

Cast off all sts as far as marker A. Place rem k44[46:50:52:56] sts on holder.

### Left front band

Work as for right front band picking up sts from centre back neck down to left side seam.

### Base trim

Using 3.25mm circular needle, with RS facing and A, knit across 44[46:50:52:56] sts from holder at left front, pick up and k97[101:109:113:121] sts across cast-on edge of back and k across 44[46:50:52:56] sts from holder at right front (185[193:209:217:233] sts).

Knit 1 row, then refer to pilsner pleat edging and work the 14 rows. Cast off.

### Sleeve trim

Using 3.25mm needles, with RS facing and A, pick up and k81 sts across cast-on edge of sleeve. Knit 1 row.
Then work 14 rows of Pilsner Pleat edging. Cast off.

Tidy loose ends back into own colours. Press pieces lightly on WS avoiding trims. Join sleeve seams. Gather fullness at sleeve head. Sew sleeve into armhole using the set-in method. Steam seams. Make 2 x 19in (48cm) twisted cords with F and attach at marker B.

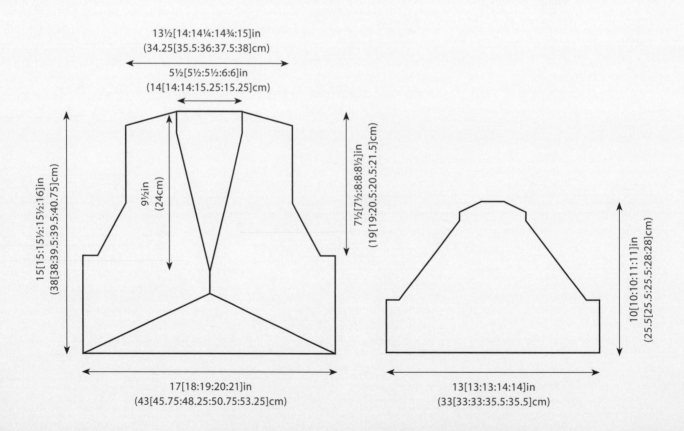

13½[14:14¼:14¾:15]in
(34.25[35.5:36:37.5:38]cm)

5½[5½:5½:6:6]in
(14[14:14:15.25:15.25]cm)

9½in
(24cm)

7½[7½:8:8½]in
(19[19:20.5:20.5:21.5]cm)

15[15:15½:15½:16]in
(38[38:39.5:39.5:40.75]cm)

17[18:19:20:21]in
(43[45.75:48.25:50.75:53.25]cm)

10[10:10:11:11]in
(25.5[25.5:25.5:28:28]cm)

13[13:13:14:14]in
(33[33:33:35.5:35.5]cm)

# Lichen chart (70 sts x 40 rows)

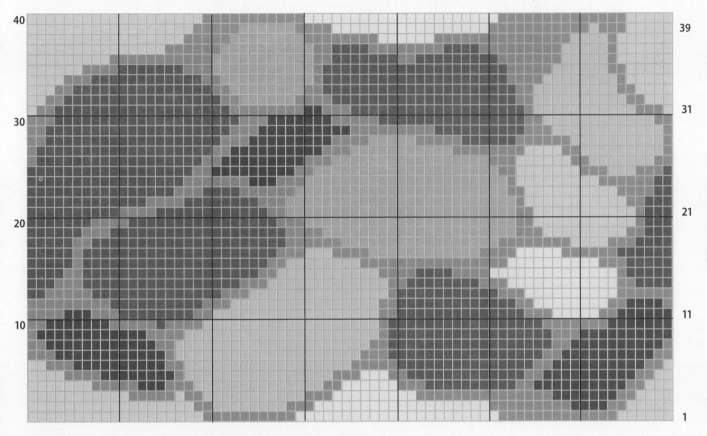

70 sts

## Key to chart

A Treacle

B Straw

C Victoria

D Bitter Sweet

E Cashew

F Gothic Green

G Spinach

H Conifer

*1 square represents one
stitch and one row*

'I found I could say things with colour and shapes that I couldn't say any other way – things I had no words for.'

*Georgia O'Keeffe*

# A Vogue's-eye view

**TRISHA MALCOLM,** EDITOR-IN-CHIEF OF *VOGUE KNITTING* MAGAZINE SHARES HER PERSONAL AND PROFESSIONAL RETROSPECTIVE OF SASHA'S CAREER.

As Georgia O'Keefe used her paintbrush to convey the beauty of her world, so has Sasha Kagan with her needles and wools. In her case, the shapes of the garments she produces are her canvas, and she fills them beautifully with colour, texture and her expression of her world. For over 40 years, Sasha has produced an astounding body of work, never tiring in her creativity, never losing inspiration, and never failing to impress with her new designs. She has created a signature look that is distinctively her own, and is instantly recognizable to knitters and knitwear lovers all over the world.

**Above left:** Anemone, from *Country Inspiration*, 2000.
**Above centre:** Floral camisole from *Vogue Knitting*, 2003.
**Above right:** Tiny Flower from *Knitwear*, 2008.
**Left:** Cable leaf coat, *Vogue Knitting*, 1993.

**This page:** Floral lace shawl featured in *Vogue Knitting*, Fall, 2006.

**Above:** Sasha wearing her Kikan cape that was originally designed for Browns in London.

Sasha learned to knit aged four at her mother's knee, as I did. I completely understand how she was mesmerized by the hypnotic stitches, the dance of knitting hands, the regular flow of yarn, the intricate patterns and textures and, of course, the colours. She spent hours of her childhood poring over needlework books and old patterns, learning the nuances of her craft and developing an innate understanding and a deep appreciation of the beauty of textiles.

Later, with the encouragement of her parents, Sasha attended art school, where she honed both her painting and printmaking skills. It was during this early period that she discovered the beauty and cadence of design repeats. She was influenced by the work of William Morris and this is very clear to me. She found repeating pattern to be soothing and therapeutic, and the sum of the whole made up by these repeats to be visually calming. This discovery of repetitive calm has been a mainstay in Sasha's work – and she has perfected her art so that her motifs tumble in a pleasing and cohesive manner.

Sasha's early work was influenced by the traditional knitting of the Shetland Islands, and by vintage patterns from the 1930s and 1940s. Her first book, *The Sasha Kagan Sweater Book*, a coveted possession of mine since it caught my eye in the mid-1980s, is a testament to those images. When I compare it to her later work, I find it somewhat geometric and the repeat patterns more static. At the time, though, it was groundbreaking, and very indicative of the fashion and harder edge of those years – think big shoulder pads, shapeless jumpers, and squared-off edges. It also reflects a more 'citified' sensibility, one that Sasha moved on from in her later work.

**Above:** Leaf pattern vest from *Vogue Knitting*, Holiday issue, 2007.

As a young mother, Sasha relocated from London to an idyllic location in the lovely Welsh countryside. The influence of her new environment has made itself known, or shown, as the years have gone by. Her colour palette is now more natural and muted, her motifs more organic, her shapes more feminine. Her repeats flow with more fluidity, reflecting the seasons she sees outside her windows (notwithstanding the piles of snow she is dealing with as I write this).

In Sasha's early work she relied heavily on her pattern repeats and on the sweater as her canvas. As her art has evolved, it has become more knitterly, and she has added more texture to her pieces, drawing from the dearth of stitch patterns that are our knitting heritage, and from the technology that has created more textural yarns. Now, instead of just repeating motifs, there are often instances of repeating motifs combined with stitch patterns: cables mixed with tumbling blossoms or falling leaves interspersed with panels of lace. Blocks of motifs might be interrupted by alternating blocks of trinity stitch; seed stitch might be used to separate sections or bobbles added to create dimension.

At one stage, Sasha's fascination with the allure of chenille was a strong presence — she often used it for edgings and motifs. At other times, a touch of angora might be added, but primarily, her love for natural wools and tweeds, and for soft and pretty cottons has won through. It's very rare to find hand-dyed yarns in her work — she is the colourist and chooses each hue with great care — and the accidental nature of hand-dyes would not fit her sensibility at all.

While at college, Sasha also studied antique textiles and embroideries. Every now and then she will enhance her work with embroidered features, and the innate femininity of these textiles has come through in later years as Sasha has designed pretty tank tops or cardigans with pleated, fluted or lace edgings and exquisite buttons and ribbons.

**Above:** Sasha wearing her Anacat jacket, designed for Joseph, 1972.

**Above:** Aster cardigan from *Knitwear*, 2008, showing a more knitterly approach to design.

Sasha's recent retrospective of her work categorizes her pattern motifs into recurring themes: geometrics, folklorics, florals, leaves, abstracts, and the witty and whimsical. For me, it is the flowers and leaves that are the most alluring. Her love of nature and her home really resonate, and it is those that I have commissioned most from her over the years we have worked together. And while most of us know Sasha for her knitting, she has explored many of these areas in crochet as well, again showcasing her talent and versatility.

While devoting her life to her art, Sasha carved a path that enabled her to support herself and her family with her work. Early on, she created a cottage industry in Wales where the sweaters from her collections were knitted for high-end boutiques all over the world. As well, she is a prolific author, a well-travelled teacher and a favourite contributor to many craft and knitting magazines in both the UK and the US. To top all this off, Sasha is an accomplished theatre costume designer — again testament to her talent as a needle artist, and her work is featured in the permanent collection of the Victoria and Albert Museum in London.

To me, what makes Sasha unique is that while she has made a wonderful name for herself with her striking design collections, she has never forgotten the hand knitter — those of us who knit at home for relaxation and to create our own unique garments. Sasha has always made patterns available for the key pieces in her collections and has influenced the designs of many others who design in this industry. Since 1986, she has been a regular contributor to *Vogue Knitting*, and I thank her for adding her unique flavour to our pages.

Women, and men, have been knitting for centuries, and I pay homage to the creativity and artistry of Sasha Kagan. She has made a tremendous contribution to ensuring that knitting does not stop with this generation. She has inspired us all with her individual expression of her artistic point of view, producing a stunning body of work that will go down in knitting history as a unique and very special collection. Congratulations Sasha!

# Knitting in colour

This book assumes prior knowledge of the very basics of knitting and sewing up. However, colour work is such an integral part of all the patterns included that it is worth taking time to remind yourself of the techniques, or learn and practise them if they are new to you.

## Reading knitting charts

Each square on a knitting graph represents one stitch and each horizontal line of squares is a row of stitches. Charts are read from bottom to top. The knit rows (odd numbers) are read from right to left and the purl rows (even numbers) are read from left to right. Squares are coloured to indicate which yarn to use in each square. It can be useful to place a sticky note or ruler one line above the row you are working on: this enables you to position the yarn ready for the next row.

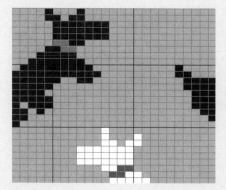 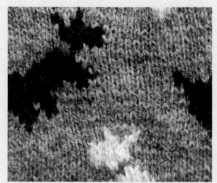

## Two-colour stranded knitting (also known as Fair Isle)

With this method of colour knitting, one colour is held in the right hand and the second colour held in the left hand. Feed yarns into the stitches using chart as guide. Strand the yarn not in use loosely behind the stitches being worked. Do not strand over more than 3 stitches, catch yarn not in use by weaving under and over the main colour.

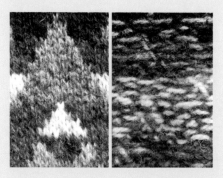 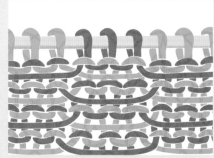

Two-colour stranded knitting, right side (left) and wrong side (right).

Two-colour stranded knitting, wrong side.

## Intarsia (woven method)

This method is similar to two-colour stranded knitting. The main colour (the one that shows on the front) is held in the right hand and the 'carry' colour (the one that will be woven behind the main colour) is held in the left hand. The carried yarn is brought alternately above and below each stitch made, so that it is woven in as you go. Use small balls or bobbins of yarn for the motif colours and weave background yarn along behind motifs. This makes a firm double thickness fabric where the motifs occur, giving a slightly 3D effect.

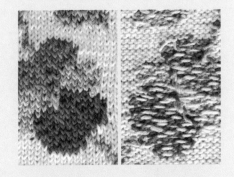

Intarsia (woven method), right side (left) and wrong side (right).

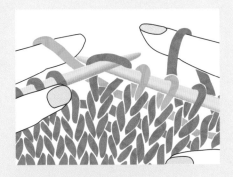

Yarn being carried below the stitch.

Yarn being carried above the stitch.

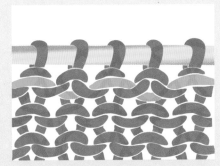

Wrong side of the fabric.

## Intarsia (linked method)

I use this method very occasionally where a large motif forms part of the design and it is too far to 'weave in' the background colour from one side to the other. Link the two colours around each other, pulling firmly to avoid holes.

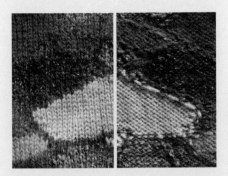

Intarsia (linked method), right side (left) and wrong side (right).

Intarsia (linked method), wrong side.

# Yarn suppliers

## Distributors of Rowan yarns

AUSTRALIA
Australian Country Spinners
Pty Ltd, Level 7, 409 st Kilda Road,
Melbourne 3004
Tel: 03 9380 3830
www.auspinners.com.au

CHINA
Coats Shanghai Ltd, No 9 Building,
Baosheng Road, Songjiang Industrial
Zone, Shanhai
Tel: 86 21 5774 3733
E-mail: victor.li@coats.com

FRANCE
Coats France/Steiner Frères, 100,
Avenue du Général de Gaulle,
Mehun-Sur-Yèvre, 18500
Tel: 02 48 23 12 30
www.coatscrafts.fr

GERMANY
Coats GMbH, Kaiserstrasse 1,
Kenzingen, 79341
Tel: 07162 14346
www.coatsgmbh.de

ITALY
Coats cucirini srl, Viale sarca no 223,
Milano, 20126

SOUTH AFRICA
Arthur Bales Ltd, 62 Fourth Avenue,
Linden, Johannesburg, 2195
Tel: (27) 118 882 401
www.arthurbales.co.za

SPAIN
Coats Fabra, SA, Santa Adria, 20,
Barcelona, 08030
Tel: (34) 93 290 84 00
www.coatscrafts.es

UK
Rowan, Green Lane Mill, Holmfirth,
West Yorkshire, England HD9 2DX
Tel: +44 (0) 1484 681881
www.knitrowan.com

USA
Westminster Fibers Inc, 8 Shelter Drive,
Greer, 29650, South Carolina
Tel: (800) 445-9276
www.westminsterfibers.com

## Distributors of other yarns

JAMIESON AND SMITH
90 North Road, Lerwick, Shetland ZE1
0PQ, UK
Tel: +44 (0) 1595 693 579
www.shetlandwoolbrokers.co.uk

UK ALPACA
Vulscombe Farm, Cruwys Morchard,
Tiverton, Devon EX16 8NB
Tel: +44 (0) 01884 243 579
www.ukalpaca.com

## Author's contact details

SASHA KAGAN
The studio, Y-Fron, Llawr-y-Glyn,
Caersws, Powys SY17 5RJ
Tel: 01686 430436
www.sashakagan.co.uk

Knitting kits and custom knitted
garments for all the designs in this
book are available from Sasha's studio
at the above address. Please enclose
a stamped addressed envelope for a
list of kits.

# Abbreviations

| | |
|---|---|
| alt | alternate |
| beg | beginning |
| cm(s) | centimetre(s) |
| cont | continue |
| dec | decrease |
| ev | every |
| foll | following/follows |
| g | grams |
| in(s) | inch(es) |
| inc | increase |
| k | knit |
| k2tog | knit 2 sts together |
| k3tog | knit 3 sts together |
| m | metres |
| mm | millimetres |
| p | purl |
| p2tog | purl 2 sts together |
| p3tog | purl 3 sts together |
| patt | pattern |
| psso | pass slipped st over |
| rem | remaining |
| rep | repeat |
| RS | right side |
| sl | slip |
| slip 2-k1-p2sso | slip 2 sts purlwise, k1, then pass 2 slipped sts over |
| ssk | (slip, slip, knit) – slip next 2 sts knitwise, one at a time to RH needle. Insert tip of LH needle into fronts of these sts from left to right and knit them together |
| sskpo | slip 2 sts as if to work k2tog, k1, pass two slipped stitches over |
| st(s) | stitch(es) |
| st st | stocking stitch |
| tbl | through back loop |
| yb | yarn to back of work |
| yd(s) | yard(s) |
| yf | yarn to front of work |
| yo | yarn over needle to make 1 st |
| WS | wrong side |

# Needle sizes

| Metric | Old UK | USA |
|---|---|---|
| 2 | 14 | 0 |
| 2.25 | 13 | 1 |
| 2.5 | – | – |
| 2.75 | 12 | 2 |
| 3 | 11 | 6 |
| 3.25 | 10 | 3 |
| 3.5 | – | 4 |
| 3.75 | 9 | 5 |
| 4 | 8 | 6 |
| 4.5 | 7 | 7 |
| 5 | 6 | 8 |
| 5.5 | 5 | 9 |
| 6 | 4 | 10 |
| 6.5 | 3 | 10.5 |
| 7 | 2 | 10.5/11 |
| 7.5 | 1 | 10.5/11 |
| 8 | 0 | 11 |
| 9 | 00 | 13 |
| 10 | 000 | 15 |
| 12 | – | 17 |
| 15 | – | 19 |
| 20 | – | 35/36 |

## UK/US yarn weights

| UK | US |
|---|---|
| 2-ply | Lace |
| 3-ply | Fingering |
| 4-ply | Sport |
| Double knitting | Light worsted |
| Aran | Fisherman/worsted |
| Chunky | Bulky |
| Super chunky | Extra bulky |

# Acknowledgements

## Author's acknowledgements

Thank you to Gerrie Purcell for having the insight to commission this book and to Virginia Brehaut for masterminding the twists and turns of its evolution. To my good friend and colleague Jean Moss for sizing the patterns and charting the graphs and to Gilda Pacitti and Rebecca Mothersole for managing the design and art direction. A brilliant team to work with.

Special warm thanks go to my dedicated knitters, many of whom have been with me over the last four decades: Chris Bebbington, Mary Coe, Glennis Garnett, Bernice Ingram, Elaine Longbottom, Linda Robertson, Shirley Taylor, Lynn Turnbull, Ann Wren, Gwen Veale and Barbara Wiltshire, without whose fantastic knitting there would be no garments and to Jean Nickolas for making up and finishing the pieces.

Thank you to Rowan, Jamieson and Smith and UK Alpaca for letting me create knits with some of the best yarns available on the market. These heirloom pieces deserve to be knitted with the original fibres to obtain the best results.

Thank you to my good friend and secretary Beryl Smith whose stoicism and unfailing sense of humour keep us both on track.

Thank you to Chance to Create and the Welsh Arts Council for helping me to create both my retrospective exhibition and this book and last, but most importantly, thank you to all my fans who knit and wear my designs. Your continued enthusiasm and support keeps me on my creative journey.

## Acknowledgements

GMC Publications would like to thank the following people for their help in creating this book:

Photography: Chris Gloag
Hair and make-up: Jeni Dodson
Models: Grace at Zone Models and Willow
Pattern checking and charts: Jean Moss

Rhoda Barker and Christian Funnell at the Old Forge in South Heighton, and The Shelleys Hotel, Lewes, for allowing us to shoot there. Emma Foster, Meryl Oakley, Rob Janes and Adrian Oxaal for lending clothes and props.

## Picture credits

GMC Publications would like to thank the following for permission to use images for the essays in this book:

Page 50: top left, Twilleys of Stamford; top right, *Woman's Own*/IPC Media
Page 51: O'Hara Burne
Page 52: bottom left, O'Hara Burne; bottom centre, right and far right courtesy of Dorling Kindersley
Page 53: GMC Publications
Page 74: courtesy of Kaffe Fassett
Page 75: top left, courtesy of Patons
Page 76: O'Hara Burne
Page 77: top left, courtesy of Dorling Kindersley; middle, bottom left and right, Colin Molyneux
Page 98: commons.Wikimedia.org
Page 99: top left, www.oldukphotos.com; top right, www.Flickr.com/Suecan1; bottom right, Gwynedd Archives Service
Page 100: O'Hara Burne
Page 101: top left, www.Flickr.com/dandeluca; top right used by permission of Workman Publishing Co., Inc., New York
Page 125: top and bottom right courtesy of Rowan
Page 126: top, courtesy of *Vogue Knitting*/Soho Publishing; bottom, courtesy of Rowan
Page 127: top and bottom right, courtesy of Rowan
Page 150: top left, courtesy of Taunton; top middle and bottom left, courtesy of *Vogue Knitting*/Soho Publishing; top right, GMC/Chris Gloag
Page 151: courtesy of *Vogue Knitting*/Soho Publishing
Page 152: top left, O'Hara Burne; right, courtesy of *Vogue Knitting*/Soho Publishing
Page 153: left, GMC/Chris Gloag; right, O'Hara Burne

# Index

Photo illustrations are indicated by page numbers in **bold.**

The Taunton Press, Inc.
63 S. Main Street
PO Box 5506
Newtown, CT 06470-5506
(800) 888-8286
www.taunton.com